PEOPLE-TO-PEOPLE CONTACT IN SOUTH ASIA

SOME OTHER RCSS PUBLICATIONS

- CBMs in South Asia: Potential and Possibilities (RCSS 2000);
- Confidence Building Measures in South Asia (RCSS 1999);
- *Ethnicity and Constitutional Reform in South Asia* (Manohar 1998);
- *Regional Economic Trends and South Asian Security* (Manohar 1997);
- *Diplomacy and Domestic Politics in South Asia* (Konark 1996);
- *Nuclear Non-proliferation in India and Pakistan: South Asian Perspectives* (Manohar 1996);
- *Refugees and Regional Security in South Asia* (Konark 1996)

RCSS Newsletter

A quarterly bulletin is published containing reports on RCSS activities as well as work of other centres and institutions involved in South Asian strategic studies, as available. The newsletter also features articles of contemporary interest to the countries of the region, and an 'article annotation service'.

RCSS Policy Studies

12. Defence Expenditure in South Asia: India and Pakistan (May 2000)
11. Defence Expenditure in South Asia: Bangladesh and Sri Lanka (April 2000)
10. Defence Expenditure in South Asia: An Overview (March 2000)
9. Sectarian Conflict in Pakistan: A Case Study of Jhang (January 2000)
8. Politics and Theatre (September 1999)
7. Proliferation of Small Arms and Politics in South Asia: The Case of Bangladesh (May 1999)
6. The Politics of Violence and Development in South Asia (May 1999)
5. New Evangelical Movements and Conflicts in South Asia: Sri Lanka and Nepal in Perspective (December 1998)

Fellowship in South Asian Alternatives (FISAA) Monograph

- *Water, Power And People: A South Asian Manifesto on the Politics and Knowledge of Water* (1997), A collaborative venture of the Fellowship in South Asian Alternatives.
- *The Nuclear Debate: Ironies and Immoralities* (1998), A monograph of the Fellowship in South Asian Alternatives.

Others

- *Directory of Individuals and Institutions Engaged in South Asian Strategic Studies* (1998).

People-to-People Contact in South Asia

NAVNITA CHADHA BEHERA
VICTOR GUNAWARDENA
SHAHID KARDAR
RAISUL AWAL MAHMOOD

REGIONAL CENTRE FOR STRATEGIC STUDIES
COLOMBO

MANOHAR
2000

First published 2000

ISBN 81-7304-350-7

Published by
Ajay Kumar Jain for
Manohar Publishers & Distributors
4753/23 Ansari Road, Daryaganj
New Delhi 110 002

Typeset by
Kohli Print
107 Radhey Shyam Park
Delhi 110 051

Printed at
Print Perfect
A-23, Mayapuri, Phase II
Delhi 110 064

Contents

Foreword

'Good fences make good neighbors', wrote Robert Frost some sixty years ago. The trouble in South Asia is that our fences are overly strong, yet they do not help good neighbourliness. The need for fences is being increasingly questioned in many parts of the world today, yet ours are getting higher and stronger. Are they serving a purpose?

Some six decades after Frost's remarks the fences between nations are steadily coming down. The European Union is integrating rapidly and border checkpoints are disappearing. The summit meeting of ASEAN and North East Asian leaders in Manila in November 1999 promised a similar move betweeen their countries in the early decades of the new millennia. In many other places of the globe passports for border control are slowly being removed. Yet, in South Asia the obstacles to movement are immense. If we are to ever develop a sense of community among peoples of this subcontinent the restrictions impeding movement needs to be seriously addressed.

This has been a major and early concern at the RCSS. What are the reasons for stringent border control? Why are they imposed and what purpose do they actually serve? Who gains and loses as a consequence? What are the procedures involved and why have they come about? A collaborative research project sponsored by the RCSS addressed these and related issues. Four distinguished experts, one each from Bangladesh, India, Pakistan and Sri Lanka have separate chapters examining a particular facet reflecting their respective perspectives. Slightly different from each other yet, comprising a reasonably comprehensive whole.

The first chapter by Raisul Awal Mahmood of Bangladesh examines the problems of obtaining visas in the subcontinent particularly for a Bangladeshi citizen wanting to visit India. This detailed case study highlights the procedural problems and idiosyncrasies of governmental procedures, whose object more often than not is to harass than help.

Yet People to People contacts are also more than visas and passport controls. It is linked to historical conditions that shaped the emergence of nation states in South Asia and their policies towards each other. Which in turn are shaped by a host of complex factors with their origin in each country's perception of its sovereignty and the perceived requirements of security. Navnita Chadha Behera's paper examines the post-modernist agenda of states that has restricted popular interactions in the region. As a result, the common people with genuine needs to travel in the neighbourhood is deterred and in all countries of the region the elites travel and have contacts outside South Asia much more often than within the region.

Shahid Kardar, a prominent businessperson of Lahore with interests in regional intercourse and from December 1999, the Finance Minister of the Pakistan province of the Punjab has an insightful chapter. He provides a Pakistani perspective of controls and reasons for their imposition. He simultaneously exposes their ineffectiveness and suggests measures to make these more efficient. The final chapter by Victor Gunawardena examines the scope and constraints of people to people contact in South Asia from a Sri Lankan view. He traces the recent history of people to people exchanges and the experiences that one can develop from there. He also suggests measures that might ameliorate the problem.

My sincere thanks go to Dr Iftekharuzzaman, my predecessor as the Executive Director at the RCSS, who conceived and shaped this project. The authors have done a particularly commendable job highlighting different aspects of a fascinating area of enquiry. It is important that the result of this research reaches a wider audience in South Asia for a rational analysis across borders.

Ultimately, it will not be closed doors and strong fences that will bring about better human interaction and understanding between peoples, a vital requirement of our times. But, an open mind and doors and windows always kept wide open and large enough, through which not merely the winds of freedom and thought, but ideas and people can move freely without let or hindrance. This alone would contribute to the development of a South Asian community, truly a major requirement of our times.

January 2000

DIPANKAR BANERJEE
Executive Director

Contributors

NAVNITA CHADHA BEHERA is Assistant Director, Women in Security, Conflict Management and Peace (WISCOMP) based at Foundation for Universal Responsibility, New Delhi. She was Assistant Research Professor at the Centre for Policy Research in New Delhi. She completed her doctorate at the University of Kent at Canterbury. Her writings are focused on South Asian security issues and international relations of India and Pakistan.

VICTOR GUNAWARDENA is Course Director, Journalism and Communication Project, Sri Lanka Foundation Institute, Colombo. He serves as Secretary-General, South Asian Media Association, Colombo. Former Editor, *The Sunday Times* (leading English weekly) culminating 26 years of journalism. He was also former Director, Marga Institute, Colombo (Sri Lanka Centre for Development Studies).

SHAHID KARDAR is presently Finance Minister, Punjab, Pakistan, and also Director, Systems (Private) Limited, a major consulting and information processing firm based in Lahore, Pakistan. Mr Kardar attended the Oxford University from where he obtained the B.A. Honours degree. He is an ACA, Institute of Chartered Accountants England and Wales. He has served as consultant to a number of multilateral institutions like the World Bank, Asian Development Bank, ILO (ARTEP), UNDP, etc. He is also the Honorary Treasurer of the Human Rights Commission of Pakistan.

RAISUL AWAL MAHMOOD, Ph.D. in Economics, immediate past Chief of the Population Studies Division and a Senior Research Fellow of Bangladesh Institute of Development Studies (BIDS). He specializes on labour and manpower economics, and has written extensively on issues related to economic migration, manpower export and other forms of population movement.

Problems and Prospects of People-to-People Contact in South Asia: A view from Bangladesh

RAISUL AWAL MAHMOOD

INTRODUCTION

South Asian Association for Regional Cooperation (SAARC) was formed in 1985 with the objective of promoting the welfare and improving the quality of life of the peoples of the region.[1] The ultimate goal has been contributing to building mutual trust, understanding and appreciation of one another's problems, and to help promote active collaboration and mutual assistance in the economic, social, cultural and scientific fields. Despite initial skepticism and lack of necessary wisdom to realise various potentials of regional cooperation as well as antagonism from different quarters, during the past decade SAARC has come a long way towards realising its cherished goals.[2]

*The author is grateful to Dr. Iftekharuzzaman for the utmost cooperation he extended in the preparation of this paper. Thanks are due to Mr. Fazlul Hoque, Ms. Habiba Khanum and Mr. Tofael Ahmed for their support.

[1] Emajuddin Ahamed, *SARC: Seeds of Harmony*, Dhaka: University Press Limited, 1985. Government of Bangladesh (GOB), *The SAARC Documents*, Dhaka, 1993; *SAARC: Challenges and Opportunities*, New Delhi: Ashish Publishing House, 1994.

[2] Innumerable committees have been formed and studies commissioned to understand various latent opportunities for cooperation among the member countries. Cost of travelling across member states has been reduced through a

Such progress apart, there remains a vast untapped potential for SAARC. The region contains about 30 per cent of the world population, and despite a low level of per capita income, 'South Asia has potentially a very large market . . . and considerable prospects for specialisation and division of labour amongst themselves'.[3] A greater cooperation in the fields of industry, trade and commerce, transport and communication, renewable energy resources, solar energy, biogas, low-cost housing technology, therefore, has much potential for the mutual benefit of all member states.

However, a greater realisation of these vast potentials is constrained by various structural rigidities emanating from colonial legacies, mistrust, administrative bottlenecks, and lack of political vision. Among these bottlenecks, the most serious are various restrictions on people-to-people contact across the member states which inhibits a flow of information, leads to a loss of market opportunities, and undermines better communication between two peoples which is fundamental for appreciating each other's problems. While economic progress depends on improved business transaction, however, SAARC viewed as also a 'functional regional

---

SAARC air-discount fare; trade within the region has been gradually liberalised. The South Asian Preferential Trade Arrangement (SAPTA) has been introduced. Greater cooperation has been agreed upon in the fields of postal services, telecommunication, agricultural research and information dissemination, weather forecasting, etc. Discussions on cooperation in the fields of transport and communication, transit facilities, use of port facilities are also in progress. Even resolution of various bilateral and contentious issues originally excluded from the deliberations of SAARC has been in progress. For further details, see, Ahamed, op. cit.; V. Kanesalingam (ed.), *Political Dimensions of South Asian Cooperation*, New Delhi: Committee on Studies for Cooperation in Development in South Asia (CSCD), 1991; Biyun, Hua, *Ecônomic Liberalization and Cooperation in South Asia*, paper presented at the International Seminar on 'South Asia at the Crossroads: Conflict and Cooperation', organised by the Bangladesh Institute of International and Strategic Studies (BIISS), Dhaka, 6-8 February 1994; Naquash, op. cit.

[3] Nurul Islam, 'South Asia: Regional perspectives on the New World Interdependence', in Ashok Kumar (ed.), *Economic Development and Planning in Third World*, New Delhi: Anmol Publishers, 1995.

organization', requires a greater degree of people-to-people contact at all levels to progress. The socio-cultural and technological context of the region adds further importance to the issue.

The information base for the present study has been drawn from different sources. A detailed review of literature on SAARC, a review of papers and documents required to obtain a visa provided the basic information for the study. These have been supplemented by insights gained from discussions with a cross-section of people such as visa applicants, policy planners, visa issuing authority, academia, travel agents, protocol officers, etc.

The paper comprises four sections excluding the present one. Section 1 looks into different problems a Bangladesh national faces in obtaining a visa to travel to other SAARC countries. Section 2 highlights the various justifications of the concerned authorities for continuing the visa system. Section 3 is concerned with the consequences of the visa system for trade and commerce. The final section contains some policy suggestions for relaxing the impediments which exist in the visa system.

Impediments to Contact

A restrictive visa system is amongst the major impediments to people-to-people contact in South Asia. The amount of paper work involved, the time required to process it, uncertainties, and, above all, the attitude and behaviour of concerned authorities cause great difficulties to obtain a visa to travel across SAARC countries. Such difficulties retard the movement of people thus inhibiting people-to-people contact. Moreover, these have an adverse effect on business travel in relation to trade and commerce, investment, transfer of technical know-how, identification and coordination of policies across countries, consultation on regional issues, etc., because such restrictions inhibit the flow of reliable and regular market information essential in present day trade and commerce. The lack of interaction obstructs a better understanding and confidence building among trading partners, and an understanding of the attitudes, norms and behaviour of people which is particularly important within South Asian culture. All these adversely affect transaction costs involved in decision making. The focus here is on various constraints involved in obtaining a visa to travel to SAARC member states looked at from the viewpoint of a Bangladesh national.

PAPERWORK INVOLVED

Much paperwork is necessary to obtain a visa to travel to other member states. The visa application form has to be supplemented by various other documents, viz., photograph, air ticket if travelling by air, evidence of financial support—sponsorship letter or foreign exchange endorsed in passport, evidence of purpose of visit, etc. Some of these are common also for travel to countries outside the region. However, the paperwork involved to obtain a visa does not have any consistent pattern across the member states, thus causing variations in the nature and degree of difficulties involved.

The visa application forms used by individual member countries vary significantly as regards the type of information sought and supporting documents required. Broadly, nine different sets of information are sought while applying for a visa. These include: (i) personal information, (ii) occupational background, (iii) particulars of travel documents, (iv) nature, purpose and duration of visit, (v) information regarding family and family members, (vi) migration particulars, (vii) sponsor's particulars, (viii) mode and route of travel, and (ix) name and address of reference persons. The specific information sought under each of the above broad categories is listed:[4]

(i) *Personal Information.* (a) name, (b) sex, (c) religion, (d) dateof birth, (e) place of birth, (f) country of birth, (g) marital status, (h) height, (i) colour of eyes, (j) visible identification marks, (k) educational qualification, (l) address—present and permanent, (m) nationality—present and past, (n) current photograph.

[4] The information base for this section comes from a detailed serutiny of the visa application forms furnished by Bhutan, India, Nepal, Pakistan and Sri Lanka. Maldives is excluded from the list since it does not have any visa issuing facility in Banglasesh.

(ii) *Occupational Background*. (a) current profession, (b) occupation, (c) name and address of employer, (d) annual income, (e) duration of present job.

(iii) *Particulars of Travel Documents*. (a) passport number, (b) issuing government/ authority, (c) category—ordinary, official, diplomatic, (d) date of issue, (e) place of issue, (f) date of expiry, (g) details of any previous passport held.

(iv) *Nature, Purpose and Duration of Visit*. (a) purpose of visit—prvate, official, business, tourist, others, (b) type of visa applied for—transit, single, double, multiple, restricted multiple, (c) duration of stay, (d) probable date of arrival, (e) address during visit, (f) particulars of earlier visit.

(v) *Information About Family*. (a) father's, husband's name, (b) mother's name, (c) nationality of father at birth, (d) name of spouse, (e) address of spouse.

(vi) *Migration Particulars* (if migrated to Bangladesh on or after 1 March 1947). (a) applicant, (b) father, (c) husband, (d) address before migration.

(vii) *Sponsor's Particulars*. (a) nature of sponsor, (b) address of financial guarantor, (c) name and address of sponsor, (d) certificate of sponsor, (e) amount of money available during stay with proof, (f) money available from own and other sources.

(viii) *Mode and Route of Travel*. (a) province/city of destination, (b) port of landing, (c) expected date of arrival and departure, (d) name of immigration check post for arrival and departure, (e) mode of travel for entry and exit—air, land, sea, (f) kind of air ticket bought or to be—single, open, return; (g) address during stay.

(ix) *Reference Persons*. (a) name/addresses of two reference persons at home and country of travel.

The above shows a wide range of information sought of a visa applicant to travel from Bangladesh, for instance, to Bhutan, India, Pakistan, Nepal or Sri Lanka. However, not all this information is required by each and every country. There are significant variations across countries in terms of information sought. Table 1

TABLE 1: DIFFERENCES ACROSS MEMBER COUNTRIES AS REGARDS INFORMATION SOUGHT FOR ISSUANCE OF VISA

Type of Information Sought	Bhutan	India	Nepal	Pakistan	Sri Lanka
Personal Information					
Religion	N	Y	N	N	N
Height	N	Y	N	N	Y
Colour of eyes	N	Y	N	N	N
Visible identification marks	N	Y	N	N	Y
Educational qualification	N	Y	N	N	N
Occupational Background	N	Y	N	N	N
Occupation	Y	Y	Y	Y	Y
Annual income	N	Y	N	N	N
Duration of present job	N	Y	N	N	N
Particulars of Travel Documents					
Category	Y	N	N	N	N
Details of previous passport held	N	N	N	N	Y
Nature, Purpose and Duration of Visit					
Purpose of visit	Y	Y	Y	Y	Y
Type of visa	N	Y	N	N	Y
Duration of stay	N	Y	Y	N	Y
Probable date of arrival	Y	Y	Y	Y	Y
Particulars of earlier visit	N	Y	Y	Y	Y
Information about Family					
Mother's name	N	Y	N	N	N
Nationality of father at birth	N	Y	N	N	N
Address of spouse	N	Y	N	N	N
Migration					
Applicant	N	Y	N	N	Y
Father	N	Y	N	N	N
Husband	N	Y	N	N	N
Address before migration	N	Y	N	N	Y
Sponsor's Particulars					
Nature of sponsor	N	Y	Y	Y	Y
Name and address of sponsor	N	Y	N	Y	N
Certificate of sponsor	N	Y	N	N	N
Mode and Route of Travel					
Port of landing	N	Y	N	Y	N
Name of check post	N	Y	N	N	N
Mode of travel	N	Y	N	N	Y
Kind of air ticket bought	N	Y	N	N	N
Reference Persons	N	Y	N	Y	Y

Source: Adapted from visa application forms, of respective countries in the SAARC region.

Note: (N) means that particular information is not required; (Y) means that particular information is required.

compares individual member countries in terms of a selected list of information sought while processing a visa application, excluding common information and documents required for travel across countries.

From the viewpoint of a Bangladeshi applicant the type of information required in a visa application form varies significantly across the five SAARC member countries. The two extreme cases are Bhutan and India. There is no visa requirement to travel to Bhutan from Bangladesh; however, one needs a 'Druk-Air Clearance (Dhaka/Paro)'. The application form for the said clearance—issued by the Druk-Air, the national flag carrier of Bhutan, is most simple containing only some very basic questions.

In contrast, the visa application form to travel to India is eight pages long and it contain all possible questions regarding the individual, his family, and the purpose of his visit. Some key categories are religion, income from current occupation, information on migration within family, and details about the mode and route of travel. The only other country which requires a similar set of information, though in less detail, in a visa application form is Sri Lanka. However, India and Sri Lanka are equally particular about 'migration particulars'. In the case of India, for instance, one is required to answer questions if the applicant or his/her father/husband 'migrated to areas now constituting Bangladesh on or after 1 March 1947' from India, and, if so, 'full address in India before migration'. Similarly, for Sri Lanka, under citizenship an applicant is required to answer 'if naturalized, date and place of naturalization and former nationality'.

PROCESS OF OBTAINING VISA

Different steps are involved in the process of obtaining a visa to travel to SAARC member countries (which have varying effects on time, cost, and predictability). First, an application form should be obtained from the respective High Commission or Embassy. Second, it should be duly filled and supported by required papers and documents, viz., passport, sponsorship or invitation letter, air ticket, photographs, etc. Third, all the documents must be submitted to respective High Commission or Embassy. Finally, the applicant receives the passport endorsed with the visa applied for.

Though the obtaining of a visa application form should normally be a simple procedure, in many cases it is given only upon submission of all necessary papers, such as an invitation letter, etc. However, in most of the SAARC countries visa application forms are easily obtainable at a nominal fee from different agents operating on the sly in front of the respective High Commissions. At times, even members of law enforcing agencies, such as Police or other security personnel, deal in visa forms.

Various market forces are very active in resolving these multifarious problems. Earlier, Travel Agents rendered such services to their clients but now they do so only for very important customers. Consequently, there has emerged a large network of intermediaries who specialise in mediating between visa applicants and respective visa officials and mutually share the fees they receive from their clients.[5]

Submitting the application form along with necessary papers is not easy. Most of the Embassies or High Commissions require that the applicant should appear in person. This means one needs to go to the Embassy or High Commission well in advance, before it is officially open, join the queue, and present the papers to the visa counter. Thereafter the applicant has to come again to collect the passport along with the visa. There are, however, exceptions in such requirements for government officials for whom their authorised agent, the Protocol Officer, is empowered to submit and receive papers on their behalf.

Besides saving the trouble of collecting necessary forms and their submission at the visa counter, services of intermediaries are required to complete the various formalities. For illiterates, their service is a must; they fill up visa forms and procure the necessary supporting documents. Most frequent travellers too find it convenient to avail the services of these middlemen even though it involves some cost. They may consider the fees charged to be

[5] The fees charged by intermediaries vary depending on the urgency of the visa, seasonality—during peak travel seasons, type of visa issued, and client's pocket.

nominal and they get door to door service. At times of urgency, the service of these middlemen are most crucial. Their connections with concerned authorities are so strong that they can obtain visa at very short notice, in special circumstances, even during weekends and holidays. Mutualities of interest of all the different parties involved—visa applicant, issuing authority, and the middleman—are crucial in such services.

TIME INVOLVED

The time required to obtain a visa to travel to SAARC member states is determined by the paperwork and various steps involved. This further underlines uncertainties regarding scheduled travel. For the whole process of obtaining a visa it normally takes about two to three days. However, it may take a much longer timeparticularly for not so frequent travellers because of the elaborate paperwork besides booking an air ticket, endorsing foreign exchange, filling up a long application form, etc. Moreover, there may be long queuing, both to submit the form as well as to receive it back.

In the case of the Indian High Commission in Dhaka, for instance, every day hundreds of people apply for visas. Thus, in the morning there is a long queue of people waiting to apply for visas, and similarly in the afternoon to collect their passports along with visas. If hundreds of people are to submit their visa application forms within a limited time the rush at the counter(s) is quite inevitable. Consequently, the queuing starts very early in the morning, at times, even before the sun rises. Sometimes people have a proxy in the queue, who waits from very early in the morning only to be replaced by the actual visa applicant once the visa counter opens thus saving him the time and trouble. Some persons have made it a business; they stand in the queue very early in the morning and later exchange their positions for a fee.

LOCATION OF VISA ISSUING AUTHORITY

Concentration of visa issuing authorities, i.e. High Commissions and Embassies, mostly in Dhaka, the capital, further adds to the difficulties involved in obtaining a visa to travel to SAARC member countries. India is the only exception in this regard as she has visa issuing facilities located at other major cities in Bangladesh. Maldives has no visa issuing facility in Bangladesh; a visa is obtainable only from certain other capitals within the region, e.g. Colombo.

Such non-availability of visa obtaining facilities in other parts of the country is a serious constraint to travel from these parts of the country to the neighbouring states. For instance, take the case of a person living in Dinajpur, a Divisional Headquarter located in north-west Bangladesh, who wishes to travel to nearby Nepal or Bhutan by road via India. He is compelled to travel to Dhaka—more than 300 km away, stay there for 2–3 days at least to obtain the visa, and travel another 300 km to return before he can finally make his journey, a distance of 100 km at most, from Dinajpur to Nepal or Bhutan through India.

Such stringent visa issuing procedures further add to the time needed to obtain a visa and also to the cost involved. Had there been such facilities in Dinajpur he could have completed his travel to either of these countries within the time he spent to travel to Dhaka to obtain the visa. The issue is particularly important for travel to member states which either have a common border with Bangladesh, e.g. India, or are quite near from Bangladesh, viz., Nepal and Bhutan. This is also important when there is the alternative to travel by road.

LONG PUBLIC HOLIDAYS

Visas are issued only during office hours on weekdays. In Bangladesh, week days are from Sunday to Thursday as of June 1997. However, many Embassies and High Commissions maintain their own weekdays, particularly as regards processing of visa applications. In some cases, Sunday is also considered a weekend; in others, some other day is treated as a holiday for acceptance of visa applications.

Moreover, unlike in other parts of the world, public holidays are frequent and long. There are two types of public holidays observed by visa issuing authorities—regular weekends and public holidays pertaining to the country of their location. It leaves very few days in a year during which visa applications are processed.

Such long public holidays have serious consequences for issuance of visa, therefore, for travelling across member states. Prospective travellers will be totally barred from obtaining as well as travelling during these long holidays however urgent their need. Long holidays are followed by a heavy rush of visa applicants and long queues. In India, it is a common feature that thousands of visa applicants rush to submit their visa applications the day before a public holiday. While pressure on the visa issuing authority is understandable, the time spent in the queue to submit a visa application form, and risk of failure to deposit it in time, is quite high. Even in the case of successful applicants, the delivery of the visa could be greatly delayed. Instead of getting it on the same day—applying in the morning and obtaining in the afternoon—it could still take 2 to 3 days.

Factors Underlying Impediments

The visa system was introduced in the countries of the subcontinent after they gained their independence from British rule. While such formalities have been greatly eased in many regions, even totally waived for members of certain regional and economic blocks, there has been very little progress in this regard among the SAARC member states. Legacies of the colonial past, mistrust among nations, institutional rigidities, obsession with terrorist activities, illegal movement of people across borders, vested interests, and lack of alternative methods of monitoring movement of people across countries have been the major factors underlying adherence to the visa system. The major factors responsible for persistence of the visa system among the SAARC member states is elaborated.

Legacies of Colonial Past

Despite the celebration of over fifty years of independence from the British Raj, the SAARC member states have yet to delink themselves from the colonial legacy. Mistrust, lack of appreciation of each other's values, adherence to the policy of divide and rule, quest for dominance under the guise of friendship and equality, and subservience to the 'knowledge and discourses of the West' have kept on dividing and redividing the people of the region. The policy planners of the region are yet to 'free the minds of women and men of South Asia from the colonial-imposed structures and thought processes'.[6]

Such obsessions with the past legacies are reflected in the kind of information sought in visa application forms used by different countries, as also in the differential treatment given to visa applicants with different political and ethnic background. Individual countries are still poisoned by ethnicity, religion, migration history, background of sponsors, and past whereabouts. The most common attitude of the visa issuing authorities of the member states is 'mistrust'; that the purpose of travel is for a purpose other than the one stated. They infer that a person is going to another country only with ulterior motives; therefore, the job of the visa issuing authority is to prevent such movement. Their attitude is that of asking the question, 'Who goes there', which was common during the colonial days among security personnel towards anyone approaching their Post. We have yet to develop the habit of mutual respect, trust in each other, and a positive attitude.

LACK OF APPRECIATION

The SAARC declaration envisaged and aimed at contributing to 'mutual trust, understanding and appreciation of one another's problems'. However, our progress so far 'from conflict to cooperation' has not been commensurate with improvements in people-to-people contact. We are yet to appreciate the value and power of a better understanding between peoples. Better understanding between peoples involves 'meeting with one another', 'exchange

[6] Iftekharuzzaman and Imtiaz Ahmed, 'The thing Called SAARC: Beyond Modernist Perspective', in Imtiaz Ahmed (ed.), *SAARC: Beyond State Centric Cooperation*, Dhaka: Centre for Social Studies, 1992.

of views and ideas', 'appreciation of one another's values and cultures', and 'cooperation for mutual benefits'. All these should go in proper sequence, and each should reinforce the other.[7]

Our political leaders in the region are yet to appreciate the fundamental value of people to people contact, determinants of fruitful contact, and various changes in their attitude and behaviour towards paving the way for that purpose. They need commitment, sincerity in word and deed, and continuity of policy. Unfortunately, these are lacking in the political culture, intellectual thinking, and public awareness building. Our political leaders operate in the culture of expediency—they support a policy while in power and oppose it when out of power. Our policy planners have not yet delinked themselves from the idea of administering 'their' people rather than serving the best interests of the citizens. It is strange that the media, both print and electronic, have not been oriented to create an awareness to promote the fundamental value of people-to-people contact in the region.

Consequently, there is little thought given to the principles and modalities of improving people-to-people contact in the region. The attitude of visa issuing authorities across the region and various requirements associated therewith reflect in this. Moreover, we still see media capitalising on issues and subjects which divide people within a country, and also among peoples of member countries, rather than on helping them to understand each other better.

CONTROL OF TERRORISM

Historically, controlling terrorism has been amongst the major objectives of the visa system followed by sovereign nations. It aims at restricting the inflow into the country of terrorists—regional or global, international criminals and gangsters, and those who pose a threat to the sovereignty of the country and stability of the government. Even countries which adhere to an open door policy in

[7]Kanesalingam, 1991, op. cit. Richard Sisson and Leo E. Rose, *War and Secession: Pakistan, India and the Creation of Bangladesh*, Berkley: University of California Press, 1990.

terms of movement of people remain vigilant on the inflow of such people.

The issue has been high on the agenda of the SAARC member states. Problems with terrorist activities have been common to most of the member states. 'Today the Sikhs are fighting the non-Sikh Indians, the Muhajirs are fighting the Sindhis, the Hill Peoples are fighting the Bengalis, the Tamils are fighting the Sinhalese.'[8] Even countries without such domestic problems remain apprehensive of other nations and international groups involved in such activities. Bilateral relations between member states have not always been pleasant. Movement of respective nationals across countries becomes an issue of concern for the authority as attested by the clause: 'if not going to be involved in any activity subversive to the respective state or government'. Such apprehensions and mental conditioning are most common among visa issuing authorities across the member states. Not surprisingly, therefore, members of the visa issuing section within an Embassy or High Commission belong either to the Home Ministry or a specialised Intelligence Department.

ILLEGAL MOVEMENT OF PEOPLE

Controlling possible inflow of people into a country for reasons such as settlement or employment has recently been among the major goals of the visa system.

In recent years, controlling the movement of illegal workers has been amongst the most serious concerns of the concerned authority. Better economic opportunities allure people from one country to another in search of temporary employment; they include seasonal migrants, target-workers, as well as prospective permanent settlers. Moreover, the movement of illegal workers is associated with trafficking of women and children for various illegal activities both within the region and outside.[9] The Visa system aims at monitoring such movements and controlling them.

[8] Iftekharuzzam and Ahmed, 1992, op. cit.

[9] Mahmood, 1997, op. cit.

LACK OF INSTITUTIONAL FACILITIES

The visa system underlines the lack of adequate institutional facilities towards monitoring the movement of people across the member countries. There is no alternative method of having any such surveillance. A system of national identification, viz., identity card or a social security card, is almost non-existent in these countries. Administrative as well as national security systems are yet to develop to an appreciable level. Political, social and ethnic alliances still dominate over nationalist feelings and sentiments. Under the circumstances, the visa system is treated as the only possible means to monitor a person wishing to enter a country.

Even for a person entering a country with a valid visa, there is little institutional mechanism to monitor him once he has entered. Immigration statistics are very poor in SAARC member states; no one would know for sure how many foreigners were allowed entry into a country and how many of them have left upon expiry of their visa. Consequently, the authority has no other option but to control entry through a restrictive visa policy.

VESTED INTERESTS

Vested interest of the various groups involved in the process of issuing visas is cited by different quarters as being responsible for adherence to the visa system. Apart from the problems relating to national security and possible infiltration of alien cultures, it is only the vested interest groups who advocate the continuance of the current visa system. These include, in particular, the visa issuing personnel in an Embassy because their foreign posting depends on the level of visa applicants, and their colleagues back home who would like to follow them in the future; various intermediaries who act as a facilitating link between visa applicants and respective officials; and officials and staff involved in renewal of visas in the respective country. They are the major beneficiaries of the visa system, who would resist any move towards easing the system. The vested interest groups, particularly those representing the national security forces, have much influence on national policy planning and, therefore, on a continuation of the visa system.

EFFECTS ON TRADE AND BUSINESS

Irrespective of the underlying reasons, the visa system and the associated problems have serious consequences for the realisation of the cherished goals of SAARC. It constrains a greater interaction among peoples of the member states, undermines better understanding between people and appreciation of each other's problems, and restricts the free flow of market information. All these contribute to a lack of appreciation of latent market opportunities and a coordinated effort towards their proper realisation. Some of the major effects of the visa system having adverse consequences for trade and business within the region are discussed under this section. Broadly, the consequences for trade and business are seen in terms of constraints towards (*a*) dissemination of necessary information, and (*b*) building a better understanding between two peoples. These two complement each other and, together, are imperative for the realisation of potential market opportunities.

DISSEMINATION OF INFORMATION

Despite tremendous improvements in alternative modes of dissemination of information in the recent past, person-to-person contact still remains the most important source of business information particularly in the South Asian region. Apart from the underdeveloped state of modern methods of information dissemination and the lack of an institutional mechanism to generate information, a particular feature of the region is underlined by personal relations and contacts.

There are particular aspects of such information relevant to trade and commerce. First, information is required about market prospects and existing government policies and programmes. Second, there is also the need for information pertaining to social norms and traditions, perceptions and values of local people, and their attitude towards foreigners. The first set of information relates to available market opportunities and the realisation of these various oppor-tunities is contingent upon better understanding and adaptation to various social norms and attitudes. These two different sets of information complement each other, and one without the other may lose much of its importance. Lack of a better understanding of the people of a country poses a serious impediment to the exploitation of the latent market opportunities.

The various impediments created by the visa system are particularly detrimental towards the generation of the second set of information, i.e. a better understanding of the people, their norms and attitudes. In traditional societies such as in South Asia, this is of fundamental importance for trade and business where 'one who knows the people does business'. Such an obstruction to understanding local people is further exerted by an adverse attitude and behaviour of the visa issuing authority and those who are responsible for controlling immigration. To the business community, the attitude shown by the visa issuing authority at respective Embassies and by officials at immigration desks at the airport are reflective of government's lack of interest in promoting interregional trade and business.

TIMELY RESPONSE TO MARKET NEEDS

The time involved in obtaining a visa and various uncertainties associated with it, have adverse consequences for trade and business. The visa system stands in the way of those for whom time means money. Business people at times need to travel at a very short notice; pre-shipment inspection of traded goods, immediate response to market changes, consultation with business partners, etc., involves immediate travel to the respective country. However, compliance with the visa system constrains timely response to such business needs.

As discussed earlier, it takes at least two to three days for a person to obtain a visa to travel to SAARC member states. Such a time is much longer if weekends or public holidays intervene. Moreover, there are always uncertainties in obtaining a visa—the requisite papers may not be in order, the sudden declaration of closure of the visa issuing office possibly for political reasons, or even the exact timing of visa delivery, etc. Such delays seriously constrain attending to an urgent business need.

RESTRICTION ON TRAVEL

The visa system puts restrictions on the duration of stay in a member country, as well as on the mode and route of travel. Depending on the purpose of the visit, alternative time periods are allowed by visa. Moreover, one needs to specify in advance the mode of travel—air, road and sea, and also the port of entry and exit. Change in either case is very much restricted though allowed. However, business travellers need flexibility in the mode and route of travel depending on the need of the hour. For example, economising on travel time in the event of an emergency, perhaps the closure of an airport, non-availability of a flight, or taking a flight rather than travelling by road, etc. Given various uncertainties in these countries such flexibility becomes a most pressing need.

Restrictions on the duration of visit to a particular country also emerge as a serious constraint to business travel. At times, one needs to stay in a particular country for a longer period than was stipulated at the time of applying for a visa. But prolonging the stay may not be that easy. Although extension of visa is allowed in most countries, the process of doing so, however, can be quite time-consuming and cumbersome. One needs to approach the respective authority, convince them about the need for such an extension and, once successful, get the necessary visa extension.

COOPERATION AND COORDINATION

It can be stated categorically that by way of creating obstacles to people-to-people contact, time taken and the various uncertainties involved, the adverse attitudes at times demonstrated by the issuing authority, the visa system stands in the way of a greater cooperation among SAARC member states. Furthermore, it inhibits proper coordination and supervision of various joint activities undertaken by the member states relating, in particular, to discussions and consultations on issues of mutual interest, meeting of professional community on regional and global issues, understanding of individual country experiences in different fields, cultural exchanges, etc.

The adverse effects of a restrictive visa policy on cooperation and coordination is particularly important for two groups of people—business people, and academia. Politicians, bureaucrats and diplomats, though they too fall under its purview, can easily obtain a visa, and are not affected by the system. They do not have to get it personally and are least concerned about the sufferings caused by the system. However, businessmen and academia who contribute to an exploration of market opportunities in most direct ways and influence policy planning have to suffer the brunt of the visa problem.

Business people cannot explore business prospects and travel on their own initiative because an invitation letter specifying the name and address of the persons or organisations he would like to meet during his visit is a prerequisite. Such an invitation letter which may not always be available.

Even for the academia travelling in the member countries with the stated goal of conducting research, studies, or meeting professional colleagues on academic grounds is quite difficult. This may arouse various suspicions in the minds of the visa issuing authority, particularly when such a visit is not supported by an invitation letter or proof from a competent authority. However, such travel is most essential to develop common areas of interest, better understanding among policy planners and decision makers, and also for the exchange of ideas among various professional groups. Negative attitudes demonstrated by the visa issuing authority have serious adverse effects on the minds of those who could , and should, act as Think Tanks on regional issues.

POLICY OPTIONS

Though the present visa system followed by SAARC member states has serious consequences for the realisation of the cherished goals of SAARC, the justifications put forward in favour of continuation of the visa system into the future cannot be ignored. Therefore, the question confronting policy planners in the region is how the existing system can be amended to enable a wider people-to-people contact across the region whilst, at the same time, safeguarding the safety and security of the respective society. Some policy suggestions are offered.

(*a*) *Appreciate the Values of People-to-People Contact.* The policy planners in the member states need to duly appreciate the fundamental value of people-to-people contact towards the realisation of the goals of the SAARC. This should be reflected in the views and opinions expressed by political leaders and attitudes maintained by bureaucrats and the intelligentsia, duly reported by the media. The political leadership should appreciate the fact that despite past legacies, a better understanding amongst peoples is cardinal to all collaborative efforts; it is the very foundation for prosperity within the region in the future. Such a realisation of the political leadership needs to be inculcated in the minds of the common people through a supportive media.

(*b*) *Simplification of Visa Procedures.* A greater simplification of the existing visa issuing procedures will be a significant positive step towards encouraging people-to-people contact in the region. In this regard, a standard visa form could be used in all the member states. The information required in the visa application form should be minimal, and of common concern to all the member states. The present requirement for various supporting documents should gradually be phased out unless called for under special circumstances. Member countries could agree upon opening up more visa issuing facilities in other countries, and issuing visas through the postal system. Where there are road links between member states, visa issuing facilities could be introduced at international immigration check posts.

(*c*) *Relaxation of Visa System for Special Categories.* There should be a relaxation of the visa system for business travellers whose activities are connected with trade and commerce, investment, policy planning, and academic interaction. Such a relaxation could be in the form of (i) waiving of visa requirements completely, (ii) a separate counter for issuance of visa for such people, or (iii) the facility of obtaining a 'visa on arrival'. However, such a decision, based on a clearly laid down principle, should be uniformly followed by all member states. Subsequently the concerned authorities should be informed about it and instructed to adhere to it strictly. If necessary, a relaxed visa system could be agreed upon and introduced by the member states on an experimental basis, say, for VIPs, CIPs, diplomats, government officials, etc.

(*d*) *Joint Declaration on Visa System.* As in the case of other similar issues, the member states should have a joint declaration on the visa system focusing on its desirability, modalities, and possible future changes. It will particularly focus on the compatibility of the existing visa system with the proclaimed goals of 'strengthening collective self-reliance' and 'cooperation and collaboration' between member states.

The joint declaration should emphasise the fundamental role of people-to-people contact towards achieving the cherished goals of SAARC, and the progress made in this regard in other parts of the globe. Attention should also be given to modalities of achieving a greater contact among peoples, and roles to be played by different segments of society and institutions, such as politicians, policy planners, administrators, journalists, news media, etc. Unless there is a coordinated effort from all these concerned segments, no significant positive result can be achieved.

(*e*) *Strengthening of Institutional Facilities.* For effective monitoring of the movement of people across the member states, as also to other regions, the existing institutional facility in the member states needs to be significantly strengthened. Immigration and emigration of people shall be jointly monitored by the member states, and the information thus generated shall be disseminated in the form of 'Immigration Control Statistics', as is practised by other countries. In this respect, all the member states could adopt a common embarkation/disembarkation card. Such information shall be computerised and published for the benefit of all member states. There could even be a regional volume of the 'Immigration Control Statistics'.

Two particular aspects of such strengthening of the existing instituational facilities are (a) computerisation of immigration statistics, and (b) training of necessary staff. A consultative body comprising representatives of the member states could be organised to supervise the institional strengthening process under the aegis of the SAARC Secretariat.

(*f*) *Multiple Entry Visa System*. If the present visa system should continue, then the member states could agree on a wider use of the multiple entry visa system for more selected sections of the population like businessmen, investors, policy planners, and academia. For example, individuals could then be allowed multiple entries into a member country for a definite period of time, beginning with six months, one year, two years, or more.

Such provisions would be beneficial for people who travel frequently in other parts of the world. It would save time and energy spent to obtain repeated visas, and enable them to schedule their foreign travel properly. Similarly, the visa issuing authorities would save their precious resources in time and material involved in issuing repeated visas to the same person and for the same purpose.

REFERENCES

Gunatilleke, Godfrey, *Cooperation Among Small Nations in Asia in the Context of the Changing Asian Political Economy*, Colombo: Marga Institute, September 1979.

Huq, A.F., 'The Problem of National Identity in Bangladesh', in *Journal of Social Studies*, No. 24, CSS, Dhaka.

Khan, Zillur Rahman (ed.), *SAARC and Superpower*, Dhaka: UPL, 1991.

Mahmood, R.A., *Clandestine Foreign Workers and Domestic Labour Market: Process of Integration and Implications*—The Experience of Bangladeshi Workers, Bangladesh Institute of Development Studies (BIDS), mimeo, January 1997.

SAARC Secretariat, From *SARC to SAARC: Milestone in the Evolution of Cooperation in South Asia*, Vol. 1, Kathmandu, 1988.

Sobhan, Rehman, *Political Dimensions of South Asian Cooperation: The Perspective for Bangladesh*, Research Report No. 75, Bangladesh Institute of Development Studies (BIDS), Dhaka.

Ahamed, Emajuddin, *SARC: Seeds of Harmony*, Dhaka: University Press Limited, 1985.

Biyun, Hua, *Economic Liberalization and Cooperation in South Asia*, paper presented at the International Seminar on 'South Asia at the Cross Roads: Conflict and Cooperation', organized by Bangladesh Institute of International and Strategic Studies (BIISS), Dhaka, 6-8 February 1994.

Government of Bangladesh (GOB), *The SAARC Documents*, Dhaka, 1993.

Hazarika, Sanjoy, *Bangladesh and Assam: Land Pressures, Migration and Ethnic Conflict*, Occasional Paper Series of the project on Environment Change and Acute Conflict, No. 3, University of Toronto, March 1993.

Iftekharuzzaman and Imtiaz Ahmed, 'The Thing Called SAARC: Beyond Modernist Perspective', in Imtiaz Ahmed (ed), *SAARC: Beyond State-Centric Cooperation*, Dhaka: Centre for Social Studies, 1992.

Islam, Nurul, 'South Asia: Regional Perspectives on The New World Interdependence', in Ashok Kumar (ed). *Economic Development and Planning in Third World*, New Delhi: Anmol Publishers, 1995.

Kanesalingam, V. (ed), *Political Dimensions of South Asian Cooperation*, Committee on Studies for Cooperation in Development in South Asia (CSCD), New Delhi, 1991.

Naquash, Nasir A., *SAARC: Challenges and Opportunities*, New Delhi: Ashish Publishing House, 1994.

Sisson, Richard and Leo E. Rose, *War and Secession: Pakistan, India and the Creation of Bangladesh*, Berkeley: University of California Press, 1990.

Popular Interactions in South Asia: A Post-Modernist Agenda

NAVNITA CHADHA BEHERA

INTRODUCTION

Post-colonial South Asian states have pursued a modernist agenda in building nation-states and popular interactions are, for the most part, shaped by state-driven choices. The single-minded pursuit of the nationalist discourse in building a nation-state has marginalised the civil society; the drive for preserving state sovereignty, national security, and the search for national identity has resulted in emasculating people-to people contacts in the region. This paper intends to explore a post-modernist agenda for transforming, fundamentally, the relationship between state and civil society, and it seeks to liberate popular interactions from the modernist logic of state politics into the realm of civil society. It calls for evolving a post modernist discourse, strengthening the civil society institutions and generating a new public culture which cultivates and promotes people-to-people contacts in the region.

The first three sections of the paper examine structural implications of the modernist project in limiting the free flow of people and ideas. This is followed by a detailed discussion on the state of popular interactions in South Asia. We shall, then, debate an alternative agenda and discuss its prospects. While attempting a general discussion on South Asia, the paper focuses on India-Pakistan relations because that is where the heart of the problem lies.

SOVEREIGNTY, NATIONAL BORDERS AND VISA CONTROLS

Under colonial rule the Indian subcontinent constituted an integrated social, economic, political and foreign policy system. The area now comprising India, Pakistan and Bangladesh was the core area of the British India empire while Nepal, Tibet, Sikkim, Bhutan and Sri Lanka were peripheral areas, important mainly because of their relevance to India's security. The situation underwent a fundamental change in 1947 with the British withdrawal from the subcontinent, India's partition, and the birth of new independent and sovereign states. The region now consists of India, Pakistan, Nepal, Bhutan, Sri Lanka, Maldives and, after 1971, Bangladesh.

Given the task of modern nation-state building, the primary goal of the post-colonial political leadership was to preserve the sovereignty and territorial integrity of the state. National borders were considered sacrosanct and visa controls were part and parcel of the newly acquired sovereign status. The havoc it would cause with peoples lives soon became evident from the unprecedented communal carnage in the wake of India's partition. The lines drawn by Sir Cyril Radcliffe on India's map not only demarcated the frontiers of the new states but also divided permanently the centuries old collective social space shared by its populace. In one stroke, millions of Hindu, Muslim and Sikh men, women and children were forced to migrate—in the largest ever mass exodus in human history—in search of safety on the *right* side of the new borders. Hundreds of thousands were slaughtered for being caught on the *wrong* side. The partition left a lasting legacy of one and half million divided families who remain apart behind the frozen walls of hatred and hostility between India and Pakistan.

Congress and Muslim League recognised the need for resolving their differences and forging friendly ties between the two states. Nehru believed:

> There is no doubt in my mind that it is inevitable for India and Pakistan to have close relations sometime or in the future . . . situated as we are with all our past, we cannot be just indifferent neighbours. . . . Ultimately, we can

only be really very friendly . . . because our interests are so closely inter-linked.[1]

Jinnah endorsed: 'Personally, I have no doubt in my mind that it is of vital importance to Pakistan and India as independent and sovereign states . . . [to] collaborate in a friendly way. . . .'[2]

But beholden to the logic and imperatives of modernity, neither could evolve any innovative mechanisms befitting the indigenous conditions of the subcontinent. No agreement could be reached on Jinnah's proposal for a common defence arrangement. Congress wanted an undivided Indian army while Jinnah sought parity inside a common defence organisation. He underlined the incompatibility of a sovereign Pakistan without a separate army and was not prepared to accept any compromise on the features and emblems of the newly independent state.[3] In the realm of people-to-people relations too, no systemic measures such as an open border or exemption of passport and visa requirements were explored to address the special concerns of their populace. People across the border were treated as 'alien nationals'—at par with citizens of other countries. Visa controls[4] were soon in place which, over the

[1] Jawaharlal Nehru, *Independence and After*, New Delhi: Ministry of Information and Broadcasting, 1949, pp. 252-3.

[2] As cited by Rajmohan Gandhi, *Eight Lives: A Study of the Hindu-Muslim Encounter*, New York: State University of New York Press, 1986, p. 185. Jinnah had envisaged a 'Monroe doctrine' for the sbcontinent's defence against outisders as early as 1944, in that, 'the Muslim India will guard so far as the Northern frontiers are concerned and I hope that the hindus will guard so far as the South and Western India are concerned. We Join together as friends and neighbours and say to the world "hands off India".' See Jinnah's speeches on 14 October 1944 andon 15 November 1946 in Jamil-ud-Din Ahmed, *Some Recent Speeches and Writings of Mr Jinnah*, Vol. 3, Lahore: Mohammad Ashraf, 1948, pp. 225, 474.

[3] Ayesha Jala, *The State of Martial Rule*, New York: Cambridge University Press, 1990, pp. 38-9.

[4] The Foreigners Act, the Passport Act and Foreign Registration Act as amended from time to time, are the governing legislation pertaining to the entry of foreigners into India, their movement and residence within and, exit from the country. The rules and procedures governing issuance of visas are derived from such existing legislation and specific bilateral visa agreements with India and other countires.

years, have become a much abused instrument for curbing the human flow across the borders.

Examples of special provisions facilitating people-to-people contacts in South Asia are not lacking. Under the 1972 Bilateral Visa Agreement, India and Bangladesh issue a special passport called 'Bangladesh Special passport' and 'India-Bangladesh passport' which are valid for travel only between the two countries.[5] Maldives citizens holding valid national passports are free to enter India for a temporary stay, up to ninety days, or transit, without requiring a visa.[6] Nepalese and Bhutanese nationals are free to enter and stay in India; they require neither a visa nor a passport.

But political sensitivities on questions of sovereignty still cause discord, disrupting the free movement of people and goods. For example, under the Treaty of Peace and Friendship (1950), India and Nepal, who share a 1,700 km long 'open border', permit free movement of nationals of one country into the other and ensure them 'national treatment' on a 'reciprocal basis'. For last three decades, Nepalese policy makers and political analysts have castigated it as an unequal and imperialistic treaty which compromises Nepalese sovereignty. The open border is criticised for having worked to Nepal's disadvantage and successive Nepalese governments, especially the monarchy-sponsored Panchayat regimes, have imposed several restrictions on Indian nationals in matters of acquisition of land, movement in various parts of the kingdom, and participation in industrial ventures and commercial enterprises.[7] In 1983, Nepalese government's proposition to impose a work-permit system for foreigners, including Indians, had become a sore point in their bilateral relationship and could only be resolved after the restoration of a democratic regime in Kathmandu in 1991.

[5] For details Agreement between the Government of India and the Government of the People's Republic of Bangladesh regarding passport and visa, see Appendix I.

[6] For details of Visa Agreement between India and Maldives, see Appendix II.

[7] S.D. Muni, *India and Nepal: A Changing Relationship*, New Delhi: Konark, 1992, pp. 50-2. For details of these provisions, see Muni, 'Indians in Nepal: Foreigners not Aliens', in I.J. Bahadur Singh, ed., *The Other India*, New Delhi: Arnold Heinemann, 1979, pp. 80-91. Also, Mahendra P. Lama, *The Economics of Indo-Nepalese Cooperation*, New Delhi: MN Publishers, 1985.

NATION-BUILDING AND THE *OTHER*: IDEOLOGIES OF HATRED

The modernist project led every state in search of a national identity. Most South Asian states constituted culturally and socially plural societies—and as is to be expected in such an ancient crucible of civilization where peoples, cultures and religions are inextricably interwoven—boundary demarcations invariably cut across communities, tribes and ethnic groups. A national identity, therefore, had to perform a dual function. It sought to unite the diverse populace divided along ethnic, tribal, regional and linguistic identities into a single national identity and distinguish itself as a collectivity from the people across the frontier. Religious ideologies in this context have proved to be a powerful force in Pakistan, Bangladesh and Sri Lanka; religious ideology is also gaining ground in India, as is evident in the growing voice of *Hindutva*.

It is important to understand the nature of a modern identity. An identity is not a primordial given but a historical-political construct. The creation of a collective *self* inherently requires an *other*, and so long an '*us vs them*' differentiation lies at the root of any identity assertion it has an in-built element of hatred for the other. We shall focus on the divisive ramifications of externalizing the '*other*' in the construction of a national identity. Such a nation-building strategy inherently generates hatred for an alien community or foreign country and makes these biases and prejudices a part of its national psyche. This is, then, used as a rationale for limiting and even questioning the legitimacy of popular interactions with other countries. Mutual enemy images of India and Pakistan are one such example.

Following the two-nation theory, the Muslim nation of Pakistan embraced Islam in search of a national identity because the partition had ended the unity of Indian Muslims and it was not easy to define a Pakistani. The identity that Pakistan sought rested on twin foundations of its inhabitants being Muslims and Indians. It is this Indo-Muslim consciousness which sustained the unity of Pakistan. India, thus remained a major element in the separate statehood of Pakistan. To counter that, Pakistani leadership constantly stressed the religious differences between India and Pakistan and the

Islamic ideology came in handy for this purpose. Within Pakistan, the debate on modernist and orthodox interpretations of Islam explained Pakistan's identity in terms of a Pakistani nationalism and an Islamic or Muslim nationalism, respectively. A number of political observers argue that it is partly because of Pakistan's constant harping on its Islamic nationalism vis-à-vis Hindu nationalism of India, and partly because of its failure to evolve a national identity on something more than anti-Indianism, that the Indo-Pak disputes have seemed so intractable.[8] Significantly, while the modernists stressed the political threat of India, in not being reconciled to Pakistan's independent existence, the orthodox *ulema* viewed the totality of Indo-Pak relations in rigid ideological terms of irreconcilable Hindu-Muslim differences, antipathy for India remained a common and critical feature of both. However, this hatred is not ancient, 'outside of history and human agency but a modern creation of intellectuals, writers and politicians'.[9]

Television, films, videos, newspapers, texts and textbooks certify stories about the past, the collective memories that shape perceptions and attitudes.[10]

With state-run educational institutions and a state-controlled media for the best part of Pakistan's existence, one may argue that hatred for India also enjoys state backing. In barring public performances of Indian artists, banning shows of Indian films,

[8] Jha argues that Islam's failure to create an affective and enduring national identity has led Pakistan to resolve its problems of nationahood in terms of conflict with India. The common geographical and cultural heritage of the two countries also makes the creation of separate Pakistani identity a difficult task, hence, the necessity for an ideology of national survival in which hatred of India has played a major part. D.C. Jha, 'The Basic Foundations and Determinants of Pakistan's Foreign Policy', in Surendra Chopra, ed., *Perspectives on Pakistan's Foreign Policy*, Amritsar: GND University, 1983, pp. 9-10, 16-17.

[9] S.H. Rudolph and L.I. Rudolph, 'Modern Hate: How Ancient Animosities Get Invented', *The New Republic*, 22 March 1993, p. 27.

[10] I have discussed the role of mass media and school textbooks in creating and perpetuating such prejudices in 'Enemy Images and Role of Media in Indo-Pakistani Tensions', in Michael Krepon and Amit Sevak, eds., *Crisis Prevention, Confidence Building and Reconciliation in South Asia* (New Delhi: Manohar, 1996), pp. 172-3.

outlawing sale of videos and audio cassettes of Indian music and newspapers, magazines and books, the Pakistani state has limited severely the public space for popular interactions between Pakistanis and Indians. Not surprisingly, an entire generation has grown up with virtually no direct knowledge and experience of each other's society and culture. The Islamic lobby, in particular, opposes any kind of cultural cooperation with India fearing its deleterious effect on Pakistan's ideology. The 1988 Cultural Agreement provoked a prominent opposition leader, Ghulam Hyder Wyne, to argue in the National Assembly that the agreement would 'destroy all kinds of Islamic and Pakistani values and traditions . . . and ultimately bring Pakistan under complete hegemony of India' and advocated that, cancelling it would save the new generation of Pakistan from 'cultural aggression'.[11] Any dissenting voices from Pakistani society advocating better people-to-people contacts are branded and dismissed as 'anti-national'.

Across the border, they find a match in BJP and Shiv Sena's ideologues of *Hindutva*. The Hindu nationalists reject secular nationalism and argue that India's national identity is rooted in Hindu culture and Hindu civilisation for the obvious reason that Hindus are the dominant majority in the country. Although *Hindutva* does not enjoy state sanction, BJP has made impressive electoral gains in past few years since 1993. The construction of a Hindu national identity casts the Muslims as the *other*. BJP's active role in the demolition of Babri masjid in 1992 and resultant communal riots extending beyond India's frontiers in Pakistan and Bangladesh points to the potential dangers of inciting hatred for the Muslim community at home and across the borders. In seeking a ban on Indian films involving Pakistani actors/actresses or music directors and tearing up the pitch to stall an Indo-Pakistani cricket match, Shiv Sena activists further question the legitimacy of popular interactions with the enemy nation, that is, Pakistan. Similarly, the construction of a Sri Lankan national identity rooted in Sinhala nationalism alienates its Tamil minority and generates animosity

[11] For a satirical criticism of his views, see Sultan Ahmed, 'The Uproar Over a Non-Issue', *Dawn*, 9 February 1989.

towards the Tamil populace of neighbouring India. The matter, however, does not end here. It also has its bearings on the task of defining the security concerns of the nation-state.

THE SECURITY PROBLEMATIQUE

Modern state security is conceptualised primarily in terms of territorial security to be pursued through military means. Grounded in Western Europe's experience, it is based on a model of competing national interests of states. In multi-ethnic South Asian states, however, there is no consensus on a singular 'national interest' of the state. In this situation, national security becomes a 'thing of the majority'[12] or is superseded by regime interests. In the first case, for instance, Sri Lanka Tamil minority militates against the Sinhala-majority Sri Lankan government's perceptions of national interests and national security. It views the military in ethno-centric terms, as *Sinhala* and not *national* security forces. Likewise, Kashmiri Muslims label the Indian army as 'Hindu occupation forces', and Chakmas face the brunt of a 'political and military campaign to transform the Hill peoples into Bengalees or its variant, Bangladeshis'.[13] Due to cross-border ethnic linkages, and moral and material support to armed insurgents, threats to internal security are perceived to emanate from the neighbouring states. Alternatively, the security problematique of a country is defined and organised by the regime in power. Successive military regimes in Pakistan have justified and legitimised military rule in terms of the ever-looming 'Indian threat'. General Zia-ul-Haq held that the Pakistan army was responsible not only for safeguarding the country's territorial integrity but also its ideological basis.[14] As we discussed earlier, normalisation of socio-cultural ties with India was opposed on the grounds that it was against Islamic culture

[12] Imtiaz Ahmed, 'Bangladesh-India Relations: Trapped in the Nationalist Discourse', in Abul Kalam, ed., *Bangladesh: Internal Dynamics and External Linkages*, Dhaka: University Press Ltd., 1996, p. 286.

[13] Ibid., p. 288.

[14] Hasan Askari Rizvi, *The Military and Politics in Pakistan (1947-86)*, Lahore: Progressive, 1986, p. 242.

and ideology. In any case, such threat perceptions are used as a rationale for restricting the free movement of people and goods even through legally approved channels.

The Pakistani government's decision to close the Indian Consulate in Karachi in 1993 because of its alleged support to MQM had a devastating effect on peoples travel. In 1991, visas were issued to 1,94,182 Pakistani nationals. The numbers fell sharply to 45,927 in 1993, and further to 24,218 by 1995.[15] The Indian mission in Karachi catered to the travel requirements of a large number of people who travelled (in both directions) between north-central India and Sindh and southern Punjab to visit their relatives, and Pakistanis originally from Bihar, UP, MP and Rajasthan who travelled in the reverse direction. Now they have to take a circuitous route via Punjab to reach their destination, and Pakistani travellers, in addition, need to go to Islamabad for visas.

In India, tight controls over the entry and movement of Pakistani nationals are justified by the fear of smuggling of arms and drugs and because of Pakistan's alleged support to Kashmiri and earlier Sikh secessionist movements. The Home Ministry and intelligence agencies, in particular, warn against the dangers of 'opening doors' and strongly advocate restrictive practices like city visas and compulsory police registration. Although there is a lack of official data to demonstrate that liberalisation of visa policies causes a significant rise in smuggling of arms and drugs, government officials believe so.[16] The argument that smugglers and subversives rarely need visas to enter another country cuts little ice. Reports about overstay and disappearance of Pakistanis are reeled off to underline the possibility of Pakistan's intelligence agency, ISI, sending infiltrators for carrying out anti-India activities.[17] The

[15] External Affiars Minister I.K. Gujral's reply to a question in Rajya Sabha on 5 March 1997. J.N. Dixit, India's ex-ambassador to Pakistan stated that in late 1980s and early 1990s, the Indian mission was issuing about 650 to 700 visas per day and servicing about one-third that number of passports of Inidan citizens who were visiting Pakistan. J.N. Dixit 'Resilt of Paranoia', *Indian Express*, 17 January 1995.

[16] Interviews with serving and retired government officials.

[17] In March 1997, Intelligence wing of the Police Department declared

Commerce Ministry's proposal of opening the Attari-Wagha border for bilateral trade with Pakistan was stoutly opposed by the Home Ministry and BSF precisely on these grounds. Similarly, the ex-Pakistani Prime Minister Mohammed Junejo's decision to open the Khokarpar-Munabao rail link was shot down by the army and ISI as a 'security risk', that it would allow Indian intelligence access to crucial information about Sindh's geographical terrain and deployment of armed forces.The following section examines how these structural inputs in the policy-making have influenced popular interactions on the ground.

THE STATE OF POPULAR INTERACTIONS IN SOUTH ASIA

First and foremost, visa restrictions and cumbersome travel procedures inhibit free movement of people within the region. This is especially true for India and Pakistan.

The visa rules and regulations under the 1974 Bilateral Visa Agreement were extremely restrictive and impose stiff conditions on peoples travel despite amendments of 1984 and 1985. Such practices include a single entry visa valid for a period not exceeding three months; a city visa as distinct from a country vis, a limiting a visitor to three or four places; restricted number of entry/exit points specified in the visa, and, last but not least, provisions of police reporting which required a visitor to register him/herself at a police station within twenty-four hours of arrival and intended departure. All Pakistani nationals except diplomatic staff, their family members and persons on official duty, were clubbed under the 'visitor visa' category which was specific—'persons visiting India to meet relatives or friends, for business or any other legitimate purpose'. No tourist visas are issued to Pakistani nationals, nor to Indians; unlike the common practice observed with the rest of the world.

---

76 Pakistani nationals 'out of the view' as most of them were untraceable. The status of stay of nearly 290 Pakistanis out of 462 persons who arrived in India prior to 1996 is also not known. *The Hindu*, 23 March 1997. For a Pakistani viewpoint on this issue, see Zaffar Abbas, 'Illegals Have Landed', *The Herald*, June 1992, pp. 45-6.

Pakistan also has a pre-verification regime, requiring the Federal Interior Ministry to sanction every visa application of an Indian national. Even Pakistani nationals need permission from the Interior Ministry in order to visit India, again, a condition applied only to India and Israel. Several measures to ease the visa regulations in 1984-5, followed up in 1989, including increasing the number of places to be visited, relaxing the conditions of police reporting and issuance of multi-entry visas to businessmen for a longer duration, did not materialize.[18] Most provisions were either not implemented for political reasons or ran aground due to bureaucratic snags.

Recently, the Indian government has undertaken several unilateral initiatives for facilitating the travel of Pakistani nationals by reviving provisions of group tourism, exempting young and elderly from police reporting, waiving visa fees for senior citizens, increasing the number of religious shrines for Pakistani pilgrims and issuing a year-long, triple entry visa to businessmen recommended by SAARC Chambers of Commerce and Industry (SCCI) and allowing them different points of entry and exit from India. The then Minister of External Affairs, I.K. Gujral, promised to encourage expansion of bilateral cultural contacts through exchange of cultural groups, artists, poets, writers, students and journalists. All these categories of people would be exempt from visa fees.[19] On 26 June 1997, the Indian Mission in Islamabad announced

[18] The bilateral visa regime was amended in May 1984 by M.K. Rasgotra and Niaz A. Niak, reprective Foreign Secretaries of India and Pakistan. Only one member of the family was now required to register with police as against the existing rule requiring every member to report. A visitor visa issued for three months could be extended for up to one year. For businessmen, triple entry visas would be issued for maximun six months. Diplomatic staff and non-diplomatic staff would be given visas for the entire duration of their assignment. In July 1985, the Indo-Pak Joint Commission agreed on further relaxation of travel regulations including exemption of police reporting for businessmen and transit visitors. The bilateral cultural exchange agreement in 1989 increased the number of places that could be visited by nationals of either country to eight. Persons with a non-extendable visa for up to fourteen days were exempted from police-reporting. Visitors travelling by air could enter at one point and exit at another provided the visa was so endorsed.

[19] See his own motto statement made in the Parliament, on 20 March 1997.

increasing the maximum number of cities from 8 to 12, to be relaxed further in the case of senior citizens and, opening the international airport of Chennai (Madras) as an additional entry point. Besides, efforts shall be made to grant non-police reporting visas to artists, journalists, students, poets, writers, businessmen recommended by SCCI, senior citizens and children. These measures are still in the process of implementation.

Visa restrictions, inadequate infrastructure and poor standard of services also account for low level of intra-regional tourism.[20] Accessibility is a major problem throughout South Asia. Air connections are limited and difficult. Promotion of national airlines and restricted competition has resulted in high travel costs and lack of international standards in services. Lack of trained manpower particularly in informal and subsidiary services is another obstacle.[21] Paucity of hotel rooms, especially budget hotels, and complicated currency conversion rules discourage middle class tourism. Tele-communication links are inadequate, poorly maintained and highly priced.

Travel by rail and road is marked by poor infrastructure, substandard travel conditions and inhibiting formalities. Motor vehicles of one country are not allowed entry into another. India and Pakistan share the longest land border but the Attari-Wagha road link remains closed as also, the Khokrapar-Munabao rail link. A slow moving train, *Samjhauta Express* accompanied by riding horsemen and running only twice a week, remains the only surface link connecting two largest neighbours in South Asia. In absence of direct person-to-person contact, what do people learn about each other through the mass media?

Print media in India and Pakistan tends to reinforce rather than question the culture of enmity. News coverage remains narrow, negative and highly selective. The press focuses on political and social tensions and highlights conflicts over cooperation in

[20] Nixon Paul, 'SAARC Tourism: Towards a Common Goal', *Skyflier*, February-March 1997, p. 16.

[21] See the theme paper for *Third meeting of Tourism Council of SCCI*, New Delhi, 9 October 1996, p. 5.

bilateral relations. 'Soft news' such as the 'process of social change and development which each society is experiencing today goes virtually unnoticed'.[22] The English press is relatively critical but, despite limited circulation, exerts tremendous influence. The vernacular press, in comparison, has much wider reach,[23] but, it is obsessed with the national, provincial and even local issues and is even more prone to harp on the parochial conflicts. Political analysts attribute the negativity of the fourth estate to the passions and prejudices of its own elite and paucity of regional expertise in print media and academia.[24] Most journalists are not well-informed about South Asian affairs and tend to rely on government's briefings and perhaps the local embassies.

News gathering is made more difficult by strict restrictions imposed on the movements of media personnel between the two countries. Journalists face an uphill task in obtaining a visa which takes as long as six to eighteen months to process. Two Indian correspondents, of the *Hindu* and *Hindustan Times*, had to wait for two years. Pakistani journalists' experience is not much different. Correspondents are given a single entry, single city visa valid for one month, to enter the country. Their application for a regular visa for three cities, valid up to maximum a year, usually takes two to four months to arrive. The practice of granting a multiple entry country visa to each other's resident journalists was

[22] Suneet Vir Singh, 'Regional Communication Policy for South Asia', in Bhabani Sen Gupta, ed., *Regional Cooperation in South Asia*, New Delhi: South Asian Publi-shers, 1986, p. 79.

[23] The vernacular press comprising Hindi and other regional languages accounts for 80 per cent of the readership in India. *FBIS Media Guide: India*, February 1996. Similarly in Pakistan, the two leading Urdu dailies, *Jang* and *Nawai-Waqt* have a circulation five times larger than the combined readership of *Dawn*, *The News*, *The Muslim*, *The Nation* and *The Frontier Post*, *FBIS Media Guide, Pakistan*, February 1996. As cited by Aquil S. Shah, 'Non-Official Dialogues Between India and Pakistan: Prospects and Problems', *ACDIS Occasional Paper*, August 1997, p. 11.

[24] Kanti Bajpai, 'Institutional Sources of Conflict and Opportunities for Cooperation in South Asia: An Indian Perspective', in D.D. Khanna, ed., *Sustainable Development, Environmental Security, Disarmament and Development Interface in South Asia*, New Delhi: Macmillan, 1997, p. 36.

abandoned in 1995 when Pakistan government unilaterally imposed a restriction of a maximum three-city visa for Indian correspondents. Pakistani correspondents have to inform the External Publicity Division of Ministry of External Affairs twenty-four hours in advance before visiting the other two places specified in their visas. For visiting any other place, they require prior permission from same authority. Most correspondents are thus confined to the capital city for the best part of their tenure, thus defeating the very purpose of their visit. Local stringers are hampered by poor communication channels, foreign exchange and payment restrictions in addition to local political pressures.[25]

Electronic media has an infinitely larger reach than newspapers due to low levels of literacy and hence it has a wider impact on public perceptions. However, the broadcast channels in all South Asian countries are owned and operated by governments and project a state-centric view on politically sensitive issues including foreign relations. Lacking a critical edge, 'they do not reveal the presence of different and dissenting voices in the broadcasting nation'.[26] Ordinary Indians and Pakistanis tend to view the other side as an implacable and monolithic enemy and dismiss the news and current affairs programmes churned out on national television as 'propaganda'. Radio has a larger reach than television. Its programming, however, is mostly 'cultural' and spares little time for foreign policy and regional security issues or stories of human interest.[27] The privatisation and globalisation of television access via satellites has opened up this medium but private operators and foreign networks are and will be vulnerable to government pressures especially on their news programming. National companies can be harassed in many ways. Privately produced news programmes on national channels can be censored. The print media is manipulated through selective distribution of the government largesse particularly advertisements. Foreign correspondents can be denied

[25] Ibid., pp. 137-8.

[26] Ibid.

[27] For a detailed discussion on this issue, see my article, 'Enemy Images', op. cit., pp. 177-8

entry, even expelled. Above all, host governments particularly intelligence agencies harass correspondents in carrying out their professional duties. Pakistani correspondents do not report day-to-day harassment except tapping of telephones.[28] Indian correspondents in Pakistan, however, face intimidatory tactics such as round-the-clock monitoring, threatening phone calls at odd hours, harassment of personal servants and isolation by discouraging Pakistanis from interacting with 'Indians'.[29]

Business people operate under equally difficult conditions. Pakistan government strictly regulates bilateral trade with India through the Trading Corporation of Pakistan. Private traders are allowed to import a limited number of products, currently numbering 573. The public and private sectors in India are free to trade with Pakistan. India has granted a Most Favoured Nation (MFN) status to Pakistan for many years past but the Pakistan government has been dithering—visas for business people involve lengthy, difficult and cumbersome procedures, taking as long as three to six months. Visa applications duly recommended by leading Indian Chambers of Commerce have been turned down. Delhi-based Chambers, however, insist that Pakistani businessmen recommended by their local Chambers are rarely refused a visa. Short-term visas granted at the last minute hamper normal economic transactions such as fixing schedules for business meetings and inspection of goods. Police reporting and conditions of the same entry/exit points further restrict the mobility of business people. Many businessmen and industrialists in Pakistan avoid visiting the Indian embassy for the fear of possible ordeals with their own intelligence agencies.[30]

Indian traders face serious infrastructural constraints such as foreign exchange and payment restrictions, and non-availability of freight clearing agents for exporting goods to Pakistan. Payments have to be routed via Dubai because most banks in India do not accept letters of credit from Pakistani banks. Land routes for transporting goods are closed. Traders need special permission to export

[28] Interviews with Pakistani correspondents based in new Delhi.

[29] Interviews with Indian correspondents based in Islamabad.

[30] *Dawn*, 23 December 1995.

goods from Amritsar. Presently, the main route is from Bombay to Karachi; it is not only time-consuming and incurs extra freight costs but also involves outdated shipping protocols that discourage even the most enthusiastic businessmen.

With regard to cultural exchanges, the traffic remains one-directional, because public performances by Indian artistes are not allowed in Pakistan. Pakistani artistes and *ghazal* singers like Mehadi Hasan, Ghulam Ali and Abida Parveen regularly perform in India and Nusrat Fateh Ali had been collaborating with Javed Akhtar to produce audio and video albums. Many Pakistanis act in Hindi films. Indian business magnates privately sponsor *mushairas* of Indian and Pakistani poets. Economic opportunities act as a significant motivating factor in determining this flow. Pakistani artistes are attracted by a large Indian market and often conduct activities in India regardless of governmental disapproval. Similarly, Indian films and videos find their way to Pakistani markets, as do Indian publications which are considerably cheaper than domestically produced Pakistani publications.

State-sponsored activities for promoting popular interactions

SAARC is committed to promote people-to-people contacts. In the Dhaka declaration in 1985, the SAARC Heads of States emphasised that 'strengthening of regional cooperation in South Asia required greater involvement of their people. They agreed to increase interactions and to promote people-to-people contacts at various levels among their countries.' This was reiterated at all subsequent summits. SAARC has undertaken several initiatives for broadening and increasing the channels of peoples interactions including audio-visual exchange programmes and a regional documentation centre on technical, scientific and development matters. Interactions among students, scholars, and academics are encouraged through SAARC Chairs, Fellowships and Scholarship schemes. In order to involve the non-governmental organisations, a set of guidelines and procedures for granting recognition to Regional Apex Bodies was formulated in 1992. These include the

Association of SAARC Speakers and Parliamentarians, SAARC Chambers of Commerce and Industry, SAARC LAW and a body on SAARC labour. At the Male summit, another category of SAARC recognised bodies was introduced. Four associations of accountants, architects, university women and management institutes have been recognised and nearly twenty other requests are awaiting ratification.

SAARC Visa Exemption Scheme was introduced in 1988 and operationalised from 1 March 1992. Under the scheme, approximately 2000 visas have been issued to date. Special visa exemption stickers, available at the SAARC Secretariat or Foreign Office, are pasted on the travellers passports. The original list of persons exempted under the scheme[31] was significantly enlarged at the Male SAARC summit in April 1997.[32]

India has a series of bilateral cultural agreements with all

[31] These included Supreme Court Judges, Members of National Parliaments, heads of National Academic Institutions, Foreign/Permanent Secretaries dealing with Foreign Affairs, SAARC Secretary-General, Directors of the SAARC Secretariat, Presidents of National Chambers of Commerce and Industry and their accompanying sopuses and children below eighteen years of age.

[32] The categories of entitled persons added were: Permanent Secretaries in Trade Ministries and up to three other officials concerned with promotion of intra-SAARC trade and economic cooperation from each Member State as nominated by them, Vice-President and Members of the Executive Committee of the SAARC Chamber of Commerce and Industry, Members of the Executive Committee of the National Federations of Chambers of Commerce and Industry, Members of SAPTA Committee of participants, all Central government Ministers/Ministers of State/Deputy Ministers/Assistant Ministers in Member States, Secretaries/Administrative Development, Urban Development. Heads of National Radio and Television Organisations, Heads of National Sports, Heads of equivalent rank dealing with the subjects handled by the eleven SAARC Technical Committees, Secretaries involved in the SAARC three-tier poverty alleviation mechanism—Finance, Planning, Rural Authorities and Federations, Chairman of National and International Airlines, Heads of National Academies and Institutions in the fields of Art and Culture, and of National Museums, Heads of Boards of Customs and Revenue, SAARC National Focal Points (Head of SAARC Divisions of Ministries of Foreign/External Affiars and Presidents and Vice-Presidents of SAARC LAW and accompanying spouses and children below eighteen years of age.

regional neighbours, facilitating cooperation in the fields of education, art and culture, and sports. The agreements with Sri Lanka and Bangladesh envisage bilateral cooperation through cultural and intellectual exchanges, reciprocal visits of educational, literary, scientific, technical, artistic, journalistic and sports associations/organisations; participation in each other's film festivals, exchange of materials and publications in the fields of culture, education and sports and, lastly, to provide facilities in educational institutions and grant scholarships to each other's students.[33]

Following the June 1972 Simla Agreement with Pakistan, fourteen important agreements and protocols, facilitating people-to-people contacts were signed between 1972 and 1976.[34] The Janata government announced bilateral exchange programmes for artistes, scholars and sportsmen in 1978.[35]

An Indo-Pak Joint Commission, established in March 1983, institutionalised this process and appointed four sub-commissions on issues relating to information, education, social sciences, culture and sports; economic, health, scientific and technological questions; trade and travel; and tourism and consular matters.[36] In July 1985, India and Pakistan agreed to post one correspondent each of All India Radio and Radio Pakistan in the other country. Indian Prime Minister Rajiv Gandhi and Pakistani Premier Benazir Bhutto signed a comprehensive cultural agreement in December 1988 envisaging

[33] See Appendices III and IV for the text of bilateral agreements with Sri Lanka and Bangladesh.

[34] These included agreements on restoring postal services and telecommunication links and resumption of shipping services and civil aviation links. A Visa agreement and a pilgrimage protocol was signed for facilitating travel between the two countries. For the text of Visa Agreement, see Appendix V. Also, and agreement for stopping hostile progpaganda over the radio was signed in September 1974, a Trade agreement in 1975, and a Rail agreement in June 1976.

[35] See then Foreign Minister Atal Bihari Vajpayee's statement in Rajya Sabha Debates, Vol. CIV, No. 7, 28 February 1978, pp. 141-3.

[36] The first sub-commission had prepared a programme of exchanges in information, school and higher education, archaeology, museums, archives, libraries, exhibitions and sports. Further steps to implement these decisions and facilitate the visits of poets, writers, performing artistes and experts in various fields were considered at the second meeting in January 1984.

cooperation in art and culture and education.[37] It permitted commercial exchange of newspapers and periodicals and allowed the posting of more newspaper and agency correspondents in each other's country.

This, however, does not depict the real picture. Since bilateral agreements are executed through state agencies they have been frequently deferred or scuttled through an executive order. The Indo-Pak Joint Commission, for instance, has met only thrice during fifteen years, till 1998. The 1988 Cultural Agreement, on revising history and geography textbooks to erase misperceptions of facts and to break the stereotype prejudices poisoning the minds of the younger generation, was held in abeyance. The protocol on group tourism signed in May 1984, allowing the movement of 8,000 nationals of each country for a maximum duration of fifteen days, while tourists travelling in groups were not required to report personally to a police station, never saw the light of day. It was reintroduced in 1989, with a new category of tourist visa valid up to fourteen days and private tour operators and travel agents approved by the respective governments were permitted to operate group tours and individuals were not required to register with the police. Due to revived political tensions over Kashmir in early 1990, this agreement also remained confined to paper.

More significantly, the instruments of state retain the initiative and control over popular interactions; government policies are informed by a state-centric approach. For instance, 'functional necessity of government officials involved in SAARC affairs'[38] has been the guiding principle of the Visa Exemption Scheme. Although the revised list includes certain top functionaries of SAARC-recognised NGOs, officials fight shy of allowing them to

[37] These included fellowships and scholarships to students in either country and exchange of educationists, historians, scientists and academicians; and art and culture, through exchange of musicians, artists, folk dance and theater groups, exhibitions of arts and crafts, writers, poets, painters and sculptors. They also agreed to participate in painting exhibitions, folk festivals, film festivals and exchange radio and television programmes.

[38] Interview with a government official at Ministry of External Affairs in New Delhi.

take the centre-stage in spearheading the cause of regional cooperation. Similarly, Indian leadership's constant emphasis on promoting the 'civilisational linkages' between people of India and Pakistan does not adequately translate into government policies. Until recently, the Indian External Affairs Ministry took refuge in the 'reciprocity' clause to adopt a 'tit for tat' strategy vis-à-vis Pakistan.[39] The restrictive, one may as well say abnormal, practice of city visas and compulsory police registration, justified in the name of national security, has become so 'normal' that Prime Minister Gujral could only make allowances but failed to challenge its very rationale whereby the Indian state treats all Pakistani people as 'suspects'. What we need is a different way of thinking—of questioning these 'given truths' and conventional beliefs. The irony of popular interactions in South Asia is that people themselves have little say in shaping their nature, direction and quantum. A radically different agenda is called for in changing these basic equations.

EXPLORING A POST-MODERNIST AGENDA

The state and civil society relationship needs to be remodelled, internally and externally. Post-colonial South Asia's modernist project has played havoc with peoples lives. There is a belated realisation that the state formation processes, marked by growing centralisation, bureaucratisation and militarisation of state structures have marginalised the civil society and, paradoxically, weakened the state capacities.[40] The nationalist discourse, in its attempts to unify the diverse people, has only caused more divisions and alienated the minority communities. Set to reproduce the power of 'nation', 'it tends to reproduce conflict and violence, even considering them acceptable so long as they are directed against *alien* cultures,

[39] When Pakistan announced unilateral suspension of transit facilities for Indian nationals and tightened transit visa procedures, India revised its own transit policy, *The Telegraph*, 7 July 1991. Indian government also discontinued issuing visas for paying homage at the Muhinuddin Chisti shrine at Ajmer after Pakistan's refusal to *jathas* visiting Pakistan for annual *Urs*. *Times of India*, 9 July 1991.

[40] See my article, 'State Formation Process, Weak States and Sustainable Development in South Asia', in Khanna, op. cit., pp. 35-60.

communities and countries'.[41] Beset with internal and external insecurities, the instruments of state have been used to raise barriers, both physical and psychological, against free movement of people, goods and ideas within the region.

The top-down strategy of nation-state building has, clearly, not worked. Obsessed with the task of creating and safeguarding the 'entity' of nation-state, the political leadership has paid little attention to people's interests and people's choices. An alternative, bottom-up approach is called for to empower the people and strengthen the civil society institutions. The post-modernist agenda basically seeks to transpose the popular interactions from the realm of state politics to the civil society.

The first critical task is to evolve a new post-modernist discourse which liberates our thinking from the limitations imposed by the structures of modern nation-states. What we need is, a 'thorough and an innovative remaking of our education', especially re-writing of biased history because, presently, South Asian children are 'literally brought up as "nationalist" or "communalist", tutored to fall in love only with the nation, they have come to share'. A communal interpretation of history lies at the root of the continuing ideological clash between Pakistan's Islamic nationalism and India's secular beliefs with BJP's espousal of Hindu nationalism introducing a new dimension in the conflict. History in the subcontinent is closely tied to the question of identity and nationalism. As Romila Thapar points out,

> a communal segmentary nationalism draws on an identity which focuses on one group identified by religion and excludes the others . . . the argument is that we have a right to be a nation-state or to dominate the nation-state because of our distinct identity. Whether it is the Muslim component of the subcontinent as it was in the pre-partition days or whether it is the Hindu majority or Sikhs in Punjab, this right or this perception of identity is based on how history is perceived. History, therefore, is modulated in order to conform to projecting an [national] identity.[42]

[41] Imtiaz Ahmed, 'Maldevelopment, Environmental Insecurity and Militarism in South Asia', in Khanna, op. cit., pp. 192-3.

[42] Romila Tapar's interview in *The Hindu*, 3 May 1993.

A communal approach to history—whether the Muslim or Hindu variety—is basically the same. Both view history in terms of a religious struggle between Islam and Hinduism and try to establish the superiority of their community. Once Islam and Hinduism are established as antithetical to each other, hostility towards an 'Islamic' Pakistan or 'Hindu' India is only the next logical step.[43] By infusing an '*us vs them*' feeling among the younger generation and imprinting an inimical picture of the 'other side', historical texts and textbooks have served as an important medium for re-producing hatred and conflict. This is only one aspect of the matter.

A history written by and from the standpoint of the dominant majority of a nation-state tends to alienate the minority communities. In the Sinhalese ideological construction of the Sri Lankan state, there is a powerful idea of Sri Lanka being 'our land'—*ape rata*. Uyangoda points out that this 'territorial possessionist idiom in the Sinhalese political discourse implies a condition of social appropriation of the state which is mediated by ideology', and it also refers to a 'collective self-understanding of a polity—a polity of "ours" and not of an "other"'.[44] Accordingly, Sri Lankan history eulogises the Sinhalese people and Sinhala nationalism, excluding the ethnic 'other'—the Tamil minority. Likewise, the history of Bangladesh glorifies the history of 'Bengalee or Bangladeshi nation' which leaves no space for the Hill people. This creates a sense of alienation among them for they cannot identify themselves with the history of

[43] See my articles. 'Perpetuating the Divide: Political Abuse of History in South Asia', *Contemporary South Asia*, Vol. 5, No. 2, 1996, pp. 191-205; and 'End of History', *Himal South Asia*, June, pp. 40-3.

[44] Uyangoda outlines following meanings and conceptions of this category of 'our land' or 'our country': (*a*) ours is a Sinhalese country; (*b*) ours is a land of Buddhists; (*c*) this is the only place in the world where the Sinhalese race exists; (*d*) foreigners have come and exploited our country, and we the Sinhalese have become poorer and poorer; (*e*) we will not allow anybody to divide our country; (*f*) why can these Tamils not go back to where they originally came from? See, Jayadeva Uyangoda, 'The State and the Process of Devolution in Sri Lanka', in Sunil Bastian, ed., *Devolution and Development in Sri Lanka*, New Delhi: Konark Publishers, 1994, p. 90.

the state of which they form an integral part. This necessarily leads them to search for their 'own history'.[45] Imtiaz Ahmed rightly argues:

> A re-evaluation of the etymology of history is therefore, required—it must narrate the history of people—it must create a space where peoples of all kinds will find their worth as human beings, and not be evaluated by the (Western) abstraction of nations and nationalities.[46]

At the regional level, a South Asian University, with issue-oriented faculties like Water Management, Peace Research, Human Rights and Duties, Gender Politics, Communications and so on, spread throughout the region, has been proposed.[47] The students and researchers here will be 'people of South Asia first and last', and would look into the issues from a 'South Asian perspective, indeed, over and beyond the modern state to which they all belong'. The idea is to 'create a South Asian mind', which would look into the business of organising co-operation in diverse fields within South Asia, not from the standpoint of nations and states, but from the standpoint of people.[48]

In fact, people in South Asia need to know each other anew—independent of their nationalist labels. Let us explain this further. A typical interaction between an Indian and Pakistani is characterised by a dual-level dialogue. When they meet in a 'human encounter', and talk about business, films, family matters or any non-political subject, they talk to each other positively. In places like Europe and North America, there is an instant mutual recognition. Speaking the same language, sharing the same values and enjoying the same food and music, they easily befriend each other. It is only when they are engaged in a political dialogue about

[45] Imtiaz, 'Maldevelopment', op. cit., p. 192.

[46] Ibid.

[47] The idea of a South Asian University was first mooted in 1992. See B.K. Jahangir and Imtiaz Ahmed, 'Reformulating Culture and Thought: A Plea for a South Asian University', in Imtiaz Ahmed and Meghna Guhathakurta, eds., *SAARC: Beyond State-Centric Cooperation*, Dhaka: Centre for Social Studies, 1992. Also see Imtiaz, 'Maldevelopment', op. cit., pp. 192-3.

[48] Ibid., p. 193.

India-Pakistan relations, each feels obliged to subscribe to his/her government policies and some kind of conflict takes place. Despite the fact that they may not be well-acquainted with the problem, they argue. It is as if they feel a 'duty' or responsibility as an Indian or Pakistani national to back their respective governments. They seem to be responding to the nation-building activities or 'indoctrination' that has taken place on both sides for the last fifty years.[49] The moment they get off the 'official dialogue', they are friendly and their points of view relate to each other. The task of the civil society in this situation is to enable the people to re-discover each other as human beings first. It needs to create alternative social spaces to allow more 'human encounters and interactions' among the people and, at the same time, humanise and de-politicise their dialogue.

Finally, the civil society actors and institutions need to forge links and develop sectoral networks across the region. In order to pursue a peoples agenda and, in the long-term, create a regional civil society, it is important for such institutions to enjoy political autonomy. What are the prospects of realising this agenda.

PROSPECTS

The civil society voices are acquiring a new dynamism in South Asia. The nation-states are not going to fade away but changing global realities and developments within the region and nation-states are introducing new categories, new concepts and new idioms of debate. The ending of the cold war, the break-up of Soviet Union, the collapse of the communist regimes in Eastern Europe and the end of the great European schism signalled the end of the post-war bipolar international system. The emerging multipolar world is characterised by growing power and influence of 'regional power blocs' rather than 'nation-states'. There is a sweeping regionalisation of economic and political forces across the globe. The formation of trading blocs like NAFTA, European Union and APEC, and the creation of ARF and Indian Ocean Rim Initiative point to the

[49] Based on a conversation with a Pakistani journalist.

future. Global institutions such as World Trade Organisation (WTO) and regional groupings have reduced barriers to business and spurred economic development. Disintegration of the Soviet Union—the military superpower—has forced a rethinking of national security in terms of the economic power potential rather than politico-military might.

South Asia cannot escape the impact of these global transformations. All the countries in the region have, in varying degrees, liberalised their economies and moved away from the emphasis on public sector-led development. Many public sector industries and financial institutions have been denationalised and privatised. Poverty alleviation, job creation, economic development and growth are high on the agenda of democratically elected governments and crucial to regime survival.[50] While the will to curb defence expenditures is limited, 'how much is enough' is being debated publicly for the first time. The lowering of trade barriers among South Asian countries has spurred SAARC to contemplate leap-flogging from SAPTA to a South Asian Economic Community. New transnational or unconventional security issues related to such problems as environmental degradation, water resource management and irregular movement of peoples and illicit goods across state boundaries defy 'national' solutions, forcing the state governments to develop regional strategies of management.

The communications revolution in satellite technology has challenged the notion of state sovereignty including the power to control radio waves and television signals within a nation's borders and drastically undercut the governments' monopoly over controlling information flows. The ability of the media to reach beyond national frontiers, across the globe, has far-reaching implications for transforming national identities. The notion of an exclusive and unified national identity is being challenged from within and without. Diverse social and cultural groups within a nation are finding a

[50] Navnita Chadha Behera, Paul M. Evans and Gowher Rizvi, *Beyond Boundaries: A Report on the State of Non-Official Dialogues on Peace, Security and Cooperation in South Asia*, University of Toronto-York University: Joint Centre for Asia-Pacific Studies, 1997, pp. 11-12.

powerful medium in satellite technology, for creating, popularizing and maintaining their sub-national identities. There is a mushrooming of satellite channels in India, catering to specific linguistic groups, for example Tamil, Telugu, Malyalam and several others. State governments are equally alarmed about the dangers to the country's hallowed cultural traditions from the imminent invasion by a globalised, syncretic Western culture represented by glossy soap operas and MTV.[51] The point is not whether the process of global cultural integration can be successfully opposed but that a national identity may no longer remain a 'preserve of the national governments'. It cannot be treated as a 'sacrosanct given' either as an abstracted, unified identity for the cultural, ethnic and linguistic diversities within a nation or by fixing, in a rigid fashion, relationships between national 'imagined communities'.[52]

A second implication is that people in South Asia are learning about each other through satellite channels, independent of the government's control. Despite limitations of reaching capacity as compared to terrestrial television, quality of broadcasts and nature of programming—mostly 'cultural' with a little time devoted to foreign policy and regional security issues—the satellite medium is playing a critical role in exposing people to diverse viewpoints and breaking down several myths about the exclusivity of national identities. The popularity of Zee television, a private satellite channel watched across South Asia, has been instrumental in alleviating enemy images of Pakistanis and Indians. Also, internet is becoming increasingly popular among the younger generation of the educated middle class in South Asia.

On the ground, the emergence and growth of robust NGOs across South Asian region has opened a multitude of communication channels on a broad spectrum of issues ranging from gender issues, child labour, and human rights violations to ecology, agri-

[51] Bhaskar Ghose, 'Cultural Diversity, Media and New Technology' an unpublished paper presented at the Indo-Australian Public Policy Conference, 23-4 October 1996, New Delhi.

[52] Ibid., p. 3.

culture, and science and technology. Several grassroots advocacy organisations like South Asia Women 's Forum, South Asia People's Action Network and South Asia People's Ecology Network are organising activities across national boundaries.

The private sector is another new catalyst for change. Conscious of the enormous potential of intra-regional trade and increasing importance of regional economic blocs in global trading, the private enterprise and business associations are setting the pace in transforming regional relationships and establishing the institutional framework for regional cooperation and networks.

Several delegations of Chambers of Commerce have been exchanged.[53] FICCI (Federation of Indian Chambers of Commerce and Industry) and FPCCI (Federation of Pakistan Chambers of Commerce and Industry) signed a Memorandum of Understanding (MOU) in May 1997. Bypassing the state governments, Pakistani Chamber agreed to give preference to Indian businessmen for imports and the Indian Chamber agreed to evaluate Pakistani bids before importing goods from any other country.[54] FICCI and its counterpart apex business federations in Sri Lanka and Bangladesh have established Joint Business Councils (JBC) to investigate and suggest solutions to cross-border difficulties for business people. They actively seek new avenues of bilateral economic cooperation, organize trade fairs and promote joint ventures. SAARC's efforts are also underpinned by a sustained and active involvement of the private sector, a process institutionalised with the creation of a common SAARC Chambers of Commerce and Industry (SCCI) in 1989. SCCI organised the first South Asian Economic Cooperation Conference in November 1996, bringing many groups of academics, policy makers, business community and journalists on a common platform. It has submitted a proposal to

[53] A delegation of PHD Chamber of Commerce and Industry went to Pakistan in March 1996, followed by the CII visit in May 1996. Recently, a FICCI delegation went to Pakistan in April-May 1997. From the other side, Lahore Chamber of Commerce and Industry's first ever business delegation visited New Delhi in December 1995. EPCCI delegation came to India in December 1996.

[54] *Economic Times*, 4 May 1997.

give a five-year multiple entry visa for businessmen of SAARC countries and set up ten Working Groups on key areas.[55]

These factors have promoted a better awareness of socio-economic and political issues affecting South Asian societies and allow debate among the civil society institutions and significant elements of the body politic. The 1990s have witnessed a spurt in non-official dialogues in the region. Non-Official Dialogues refer to a host of activities including various kinds of meetings, training, research programmes, exchanges and workshops which focus on issues ranging from economic cooperation and social issues through to political security matters.[56] The criteria is not the kind of setting but the intention to discuss sensitive issues across the borders. Let us make a distinction between track-two and track-three efforts.

By track-two is meant policy related discussions which are technically non-governmental but have the explicit intention of influencing or informing public policy. As a form of shadow diplomacy, the track-two dialogues provide a second line of communication between conflicting states and serve as 'testing grounds' for new policy initiatives. Neemrana dialogue between India and Pakistan is a case in point. Track-two dialogues have a close connection to government, either through the participation of government officials in their personal and private capacities or through their direct channels of communication in government circles. They have been used occasionally to explore alternatives for conflict management at a non-governmental level, preceding or setting the foundations for, negotiations at a formal governmental level. A related activity has been the preparation of technical materials and studies in support of alternative policy options. Decision-makers at the highest level in India, Pakistan and Bangladesh have acknowledged and appreciated the significance of some dialogues including the Ganga-Brahmaputra-Meghna water dialogues

[55] These include trade, investment, energy, science and technology, travel and tourism, telecommunications, business information and data networking, human resources development, social dimensions of business development and women entrepreneurs. *The Nation*, 27 April 1997.

[56] I have borrowed heavily from my co-authored monograph, 'Beyond Boundaries' to write this section, op. cit.

involving India, Bangladesh and Nepal and India-Bangladesh dialogue on trade issues which eventually produced a list of twenty-two items for open trade and played a modest but important role in the events leading up to the successful conclusion of the Ganga Waters Treaty.

Track-three dialogues, principally 'people-to-people' initiatives, also focus on contemporary policy issues but these explicitly function apart from, or beyond, governments. They are composed of individuals and groups looking across national frontiers and states, aiming to build constituencies for peace which can question conventional practices and beliefs and present alternatives to official government positions. These rarely have direct access to the relevant foreign offices but, instead, aim to change public attitudes and mobilise public pressure on their respective governments to resolve differences and disputes. Several NGO activists, trade unionists, artistes, journalists and intellectuals have, for example, sought to create a mass-based channel for bilateral interactions between India and Pakistan through Pakistan-India People's Forum for Peace & Democracy. In India, the forum has regional chapters in Mumbai, Patna, Delhi, Varanasi, Chennai and Hyderabad. Pakistani chapters are located in Karachi, Lahore, Quetta, Peshawar, Islamabad and Hyderabad. The Forum has broken new ground in bringing more than one hundred delegates from each country to its annual conventions. At the convention in December 1996, nearly one hundred and seventy Pakistani delegates created a record by walking across the Wagah border and travelling by train to Calcutta.

Some dialogues are born out of personal links across the borders. Examples include, a network of Indian and Pakistani former students of the Royal Indian Military College (RIMC) and Doon School Old Boys network. Other issue-specific, multilateral dialogues are designed to suggest directions and policy options for regional institutions, particularly SAARC. The Independent Group for South Asian Cooperation (IGSAC) focuses mainly on economic issues. Coalition for Action on South Asian Co-operation (CASAC) promotes interactions with like-minded groups in the fields of environment, media, economics and human rights. South Asia

Media Association (SAMA) and NAM Media engages journalists in research and discussion on media-related issues. South Asia Human Rights Documentation Centre maintains an informal network of partner organisations in South Asian countries and attempts to develop common approaches to human rights issues. The Centre has addressed issues relating to prisoner exchanges between South Asian countries, children's rights, communalism, labour rights and women's rights. Dialogues focusing on unconventional security issues include Climate Action Network, conducting projects on environmental security, and on a Himalayan Drainage Ecosystems programme. Duryog Nivaran is a South Asian initiative on disaster management that seeks to explore the linkages between natural and man-made disasters. Several dialogues promote cultural interactions in the region. These include Ajoka group, Centre for Asian Theatre and South Asian Youth Association for Regional Cooperation.

Last but not least, dialogues like the Summer Workshop on Science, Technology and Arms Control and the Winter School on Non-Military Sources of Conflict in South Asia involve younger South Asians. The emergence of a new generation of Indians and Pakistanis—'the Midnight's Grandchildren',[57] is of special significance. They do not carry the psycho-logical baggage of the partition trauma. The third generation has been exposed to a wide variety of international influences through films, music, travel and, more recently, satellite television. There is a growing trend of an expatriate generation of students returning home with stronger commitment to South Asian connections and possibilities. The third generation does not, of course, constitute a monolithic social group. 'Widespread differences in upbringing, education, social mobility and regional and ethnic preferences separate them to a great degree from peers in their own countries.'[58] The post-1971 generation of educated urban middle class is more cosmopolitan and liberal in outlook; they neither perceive the 'other side' as 'the

[57] Ameen Jan, 'A New Generation, and Future, for South Asia', *The Christian Science Monitor*, 22 August 1997.

[58] Aquil Shah, op. cit., p. 6.

root of all evil' nor are they prepared to 'sacrifice the future to get even'.[59]

Contact is also being established between the fourth generation of Indians and Pakistanis. The school children of Karachi and Bombay interact through a letter exchange programme called 'Peace Pals'.[60] 'This letter is about making peace' by twelve-year old Ashwini Kamath, strikes a chord in ninth grader Haider Ali's letter—'I am writing to establish cordial relations between us'. The cynics may dismiss it as a naive and inconsequential exercise. But an early realisation among the third and fourth generation of Indians and Pakistanis, of the futility of hostility, is of far-reaching import as Haleem, another child, says: 'We are the future. We will grow up and become the adults . . . and because of this interaction, we will pass on a more positive attitude.'[61]

There are more than forty dialogue channels in South Asia and about a dozen more outside the region in which South Asian states participate on a regular basis.[62] Critics point out that the non-official dialogues have not produced any dramatic breakthroughs on contentious regional issues nor brought any qualitative transformation in the calculus of bilateral and regional cooperation. They have not had the same kind of cumulative effect or achieved a systematic influence on governmental thinking and interactions as in the neighbouring areas. Non-official dialogues are still at a comparatively nascent stage and it is premature to expect quick

[59] Cohen argues that the younger officers of Pakistan army are moving towards a position that a 'victory' that also destroys one's own country does not make military, political or moral sense. See, Stephen P. Cohen, 'South Asia: The Origins of War and the Conditions for Peace', in Roger E. Kanet, ed., *Regional Conflicts and Conflict Resolution*, ACDIS, 1995, p. 138. Waslekar points out the generational gap in track-two dialogues. Most retired army or government officials tend to be obsessed with problems in terms of ten or twenty years earlier and most young people look at problems in terms of what it means for their future. Sundeep Waslekar, 'Track-Two Diplomacy in South Asia', *ACDIS Occasional Paper*, October 1995, p. 8.

[60] Ayesha Ali Murshed, 'Understanding Thy Neighbour', *Newsline*, May 1997, pp. 67-8.

[61] Ibid.

[62] For details of these dialogues, see 'Beyond Boundaries', op. cit.

results, especially when formal diplomatic efforts are, and have been for the last five decades, still grappling with the same issues.[63] Besides, motives of foreign-funded dialogues are viewed with suspicion and Western origins of track-two terminology are used to make a case for proving their irrelevance in the region or castigating them as an 'artificial imposition from outside'. While this may be true for a mechanical application of specific track-two initiatives, rooted in the cold war experience, to the South Asian region, but to debunk the very phenomenon of non-official dialogues amounts to throwing the baby out with the bathwater.

The overall value of these dialogues has to be measured against a different set of standards. They have promoted exchanges and coalition building among like-minded individuals and groups and helped cement new sectoral networks among the private sector and citizens groups which operate across borders and share the general goal of building a more peaceful and cooperative South Asia. Viewed from the people's perspective, the dialogues have been valuable in stimulating cross-national interactions, reshaping opinions and creating a sense of empowerment among the participants. It is often the intangibles such as the 'psychological release of speaking with the enemy', where 'the real value of the dialogues', lies especially in the early stages of the peace process.[64]

CONCLUSION

Non-official dialogues are only part of the larger process of promoting popular interactions by strengthening the civil society institutions. What is at stake is a fundamental shift in the societal equations; they are bound to face stiff opposition from vested interests and lobbies. Governments attitude towards non-official dialogue processes, in particular, varies from indifference to hostility. Officials are predictably alarmed by the emergence of powerful and influential non-governmental organisations. Some

[63] Ibid., p. 27.
[64] Ibid., p. 28.

policy makers expressed 'disinterest bordering on contempt for the involvement of outsiders described by an official as "naive meddlers and amateurs" lacking the skills and information to manage sensitive issues'.[65] Others debunk them as harmful to the 'national interests'. The Pakistan-India Forum's Convention at New Delhi was criticised by Pakistan's Foreign Office, Ministry of Information, and members of the Kashmir Committee as 'inappropriate and questionable [in its] timing, tenor and size'. There are, moreover, constituencies in governments, especially in the armed forces and security apparatuses, who have a vested interest in maintaining high levels of tension.

But the people's mood is undergoing a positive transformation. The results of two public opinion polls held on the fiftieth anniversary of independence by *Herald* and *India Today*, two leading current affairs magazines in Pakistan and India respectively, speak volumes. In the *Herald* poll, 59 per cent Pakistanis, across the regional divide, supported friendlier ties with India. In the *India Today* poll, 45 per cent people wanted the Indian government to take initiatives in improving relations with Pakistan.[66] In an earlier poll by *Times of India* in India, 60 per cent favoured closer cultural contacts and people-to-people relations with Pakistan and 56 per cent respondents felt that India should seek to improve trade and economic relations with Pakistan.[67] Examples of more specific initiatives by common citizens include, in early 1990, a joint statement by fifty-four eminent citizens of India and Pakistan pleading for peace and urging the governments to take immediate steps to avert risks of a mutually destructive military confrontation. Also, in June 1996 Indian and Pakistani members of the non-governmental observer team in Bangladesh issued the 'Dhaka Statement' which supported an unconditional dialogue between New Delhi and Islamabad. It urged them to tackle the 'less tractable' issues first without minimising the gravity of more sensitive problems. Peace

[65] Ibid., 32.

[66] *Herald*, Annual 1997, p. 167; *India Today*, 31 August, p. 52.

[67] *Times of India*, 6 April 1995.

marchers from India have, for last two years, led a candle light procession in a gesture of friendship for people of Pakistan, to the Attari-Wagah border check post, on 15 August. People are clearly beginning to assert their choices and ultimately, they wield the power to realise the post-modernist agenda of popular interactions in South Asia.

APPENDIX I

AGREEMENT BETWEEN THE GOVERNMENT OF INDIA AND THE GOVERNMENT OF THE PEOPLES'S REPUBLIC OF BANGLADESH REGARDING PASSPORT AND VISA

Dacca, 3 August 1972

The Government of People's Republic of Bangladesh

And

The Government of the Republic of India

HAVE agreed to introduce a Passport/Visa System to regulate travel between the two countries. This system will come into effect from 1 September 1972.

A. PASSPORT

A passport called "Bangladesh Special Passport" and a passport called "India-Bangladesh Passport" will be issued by the Government of Bangladesh and the Government of India respectively which will be valid for travel only between the two countries.

An International Passport issued by the two Governments to their respective nationals with appropriate endorsement will also be valid for travel only between the two countries.

B. VISAS

Nationals of Bangladesh and India travelling to the other country will be required to have a valid visa.

Visas shall be granted by the competent authorities designated by the respeetive governments. Visas will be given gratis.

(I) Categories of Visas: There will be the following categories of visas:

(a) Diplomatic and official visa—These will be granted in accordance with international convention and practice.

(b) Short-term single entry visa—This type of visa is to be availed of within one month of its issue and shall be valid for stay upto three months from the date of entry. Such visas may be extended in appropriate cases for a further maximum period of three months without any requirement of registration and residential permit.

(c) Long term multiple journey visa—This type of visa may be granted to nationals of the two countries in appropriate cases. Such visa will have to be availed of within one month of its issue and shall be valid for stay upto maximum period of one year from the date of first entry. This visa will be valid for more than one journey: the number of journeys may be specified on the visa by the issuing authority.

(d) Transit visa—Nationals of one country transiting through the other country by land, river or air routes will be required to have a transit visa to be availed of within one month of its issue, valid for a stay upto a maximum period of 15 days from the date of entry. There will be no visa required for direct transit through airport/ seaport.

(e) Re-entry visa—Nationals of one country on a visit to the other country on a valid visa may be granted re-entry as appropriate.

(II) All categories of visas will be valid for travel to and stay in any part of the country concerned except for those areas designated by the respective Government as Protected, Restricted or Prohibited Areas.

(III) Issuing Authorities: Diplomatic Missions and Consular Posts of the two countries and other agencies designated by the two Governments will be authorized to issue visas. A list of visa issuing authorities designated by one Government will be communicated to the other Government through normal diplomatic channels.

C. REGISTRATION

National of one country visiting the other country on a valid visa who wish to stay for a continuous period exceeding six months will be required to register with the appropriate authorities and obtain residential permit.

D. SEAMEN

Seamen of both the countries holding a valid Continuous Discharge Certificate (CDC) bearing a photograph and other prescribed particulars will be accorded the following facilities:

(a) A seamen of one country visiting the port of other country as a member of the crew of the ship which brings him need not hold a passport or a visa. He will be issued a landing permit on deposit of his C.D.C., if he wishes to land.
(b) A seaman who arrives at a port in the other country as a member of the crew of the ship which brings him and who is discharged at the port, will not require passport/visa. He will be issued a landing permit for a pecified period and will also be allowed to travel to the country of which he is a national.
(c) A Bangladesh seaman, who has signed on Bn Articles and desires to join his ship at an Indian port, will require an Indian visa on his CDC. Similarly, an Indian seaman, who has signed on Indian Articles and desires to join his ship at Bangladesh port, will require a Bn visa on his CDC.
(d) In all other cases, a seaman will be subject to the normal requirements governing travel between the two countries.

E. INLAND WATER TRANSPORT PERSONNEL

Ranking personnel and ratings of an island vessel belonging to one country visiting or transiting through the other country will call the designated checkpoints on the route. Such personnel will not require a transit visa.

F. ENTRY INTO BANGLADESH AND INDIA

Bangladesh and Indian nationals holding valid travel documents will be required to leave one country and enter the other only through the designated checkpoints. Both sides agree that corresponding check-post of the two countreis should be located as near as possible to each other.

G. BORDER TRADE

Holders of Border Trade Permits issued by the two Governments to their respective nationals under the provisions of the Trade agreement of March 1972 between the two countries will be exempt from passport and visa requirements for the purposes of border trade as stipulated in their permits.

H. BANGLADSH NATIONALS IN INDIA ON 1 SEPTEMBER 1972 AND INDIAN NATIONALS IN BANGLADESH ON 1 SEPTEMBER 1972

Nationals of Bangladesh and India who are already in India and Bangladesh respectively when the above arrangements came into force can continue to stay in the country concerned on the basis of their existing travel documents upto 30 September 1972.

I. REVIEW

Both sides agree that the Arrangements set out above will be reviewed after a period of one year or as and when desired by either Party, at one month's notice.

On behalf of the Government of the Republic of India	On behalf of the Government of the People's Republic of Bangladesh
Sd/-	Sd/-
Avtar Singh Secretary (West) Ministry of External Affairs Government of the Republic of India	Taslim Ahmed Secretary Ministry of Home Affairs Government of the People's Republic of Bangladesh

APPENDIX II

EXCHANGE OF LETTERS CONSTITUTING AN AGREEMENT BETWEEN THE GOVERNMENT OF INDIA AND THE GOVERNMENT OF THE REUBLIC OF MALDIVES REGARDING ABOLITION OF VISAS

Male, 11 March 1979

EMBASSY OF INDIA TO THE
REPUBLIC OF MALDIVES

MALE

No. MAL/406/2/76 March 11, 1979

EXCELLENCY,

I have the honour to refer to the discussions held from time to time between our two Governments on measures to facilitate travel between the two countries and to set out below the understanding aimed at between our two Governments in this regard:

(i) It is agreed that citizens of India and citizens of the Maldives holding valid national passports shall be free to enter Maldives and India respectively at any border crossing place authorised for international passenger traffic for the purpose of temporary stay for a period utp 90 days or for transit, without being required to obtain a visa. This period of 90 days shall include the period of stay if any during the preceeding six months.

(ii) It is further understood that the waiver of visa requirements does not exempt citizens of India and citizens of Maldives coming to Maldives and India respectively from the obligation to comply with the laws and regulations in force in Maldives and in India respectively concerning the entry into, movement within and residence—temporary or permanent in that country. Nor are they allowed to take up employment, set up any business, or exercise any profession, paid or unpaid, in either country, without the consent of the government and in conformity with the laws and regulations of the respective country. This requirement, however, shall not apply to businessmen or business delegations from either country going to other to conclude business agreements, contracts or other business transactions and to conduct negotiations with their counterparts.

(iii) The authorities of wither country reserve the right to refuse entry or stay in their country to persons considered undesirable.

(iv) Either Government may temporarily suspend the foregoing provisions in whole or in part for reasons of public order or public health. Such suspension shall, as far as possible, be resorted to after prior consultations with the other Government but shall, in any case, be notified to the other Government immediately through diplomatic channel.

(v) The present understanding may be terminated by either Government by notifying the other Government in writing of its intention to that effect and shall stand terminated at the expiry of ninety days from the date of receipt by the other Government of such notification.

2 If the understanding as set out above is acceptable to the Government of Maldives, I have the honour to request you to kindly confirm such acceptance and to suggest that this letter and your reply to that effect shall constitute an Agreement between the two Governments, which shall enter into force on the date of your letter of reply.

Please accept the assurances of my highest consideration.

Yours sincerly

Sd/-

THOMAS ABRAHAM

H.E. Mr. FATHULLA JAMEEL
Minister of External Affairs
Republic of Maldives
Male

(SEAL)

THE MINSITER OF EXTERNAL AFFAIRS
MALE

Your EXCELLENCY, 11 March 1979

I have the honour to acknowledge receipt of your letter No. MAL/406/2/76 dated March 11, 1979 which reads as follows:

[*Not reproduced*]

I have the honour to confirm that the above correctly sets out the Agreement reached between us. Your letter and my reply thereto shall constitute an Agreement between the Government of India and the Government of the Republic of Maldives.

Please accept, your Excellency, the assurance of my highest consideration.

Yours sincerely
Sd/-

FATHULLA JAMEEL
Minister of External Affairs

H.E. Mr. THOMAS ABRAHAM
Ambassador of India

APPENDIX III

CULTURAL AGREEMENT BETWEEN THE GOVERNMENT OF INDIA AND THE GOVERNMENT OF THE REPUBLIC OF SRI LANKA

New Delhi, 29 November 1977

Inspired by the common desire tc establish and develop closer cultural relations between the two countries in the spirit of the high ideals of the Constitution of the United Nations Educational, Scientific and Cultural Organization; and

DESIROUS OF promoting and developing such relations and understanding in every possible manner, especially in the realm of art, culture, education and sports;

HAVE AGREED to conclude the following Agreement:

Article 1

The Contracting Parties shall facilitate and encourage cooperation between the two countries in the fields of art and culture, education including academic activity therein, and sports and games in order to contribute towards a better knowledge of their respective cultures and activities in these fields.

Article 2

The cooperation envisaged in Article 1 of this Agreement shall be realised by the Contracting Partis, *inter alia*, through:

(a) cultural and intellectual exchanges;
(b) reciprocal visits of representatives of educational, literary, and sports associations/organizations and participation in congresses, conferences, symposia and seminars;
(c) participation in each other's international film festivals;
(d) exchange of materials in the fields of culture, education, sports, translation and exchange of educational, cultural and sports, publications and wherever possible, exchange of art specimens and exhibitions; and
(e) reciprocal facilities to archaeologists to gain experience and training in regard to excavations, preservation and display of archaeological finds and exchange of specimens, replicas or casts.

Article 3

Each Contracting party shall endeavour to provide facilities and scholarships to students of the other country seeking to study in its institutions of higher education.

Article 4

The Contracting Parties shall examine the diplomas, certificates and university degrees granted by the other Contracting Party with a view to arriving at their equivalence.

Article 5

The Contracting Parties shall encourage visits of sports teams between the two countries and shall facilitate their stay and movements in their respective territories.

Article 6

The Contracting Parties shall, to the extent possible, ensure that textbooks prescribed for their educational institutions, particularly those relating to history and geography, do not contain any error or misrepresentation of facts about each other's country.

Article 7

For the purpose of fulfilment of the objectives of the present Agreement, a Joint Committee may be established by the Contracting Parties, as and when considered necessary, consisting of an equal number of representatives of the two Governments. The Joint Committee shall meet as agreed upon between the Contracting Parties at the request of either of them, alternately in New Delhi and Colombo.

The Joint Committee shall be responsible for:

(a) drawing up of an annual programme of activities under this Agreement;
(b) keeping under periodical review the working of the Agreement in the two countires;
(c) recommending to the Contracting Party concerned any items of interest to that party in the field within the scope of this Agreement; and
(d) generally advising the Contracting Party concerned as to the manner in which the working of the Agreement may be improved upon.

Article 8

The present Agreement shall come into force upon exchange of Instruments of its Ratification between the Contracting Parties. It shall remain in force for a period of five years and thereafter shall be renewed automatically for further periods of five years each time, unless either Contracting Party gives to the other party a written notice, six months in advance, of its intention to terminate the Agreement.

IN WITNESS WHEREOF, the duly authorised representatives of the Contracting Parties have signed the present Agreement and have affixed their seals thereto.

DONE at New Delhi on this day of Eighth Agrahayana, 1899 (SAKA) corresponding to this Kuja Dina, third day of Awa of the month of IL, Buddha Varsha 2521 and to the 29th day of November, 1977 (A.D.) in six originals two each in Hindi, Sinhala and English languages, all the texts being equally authentic provided that in case of doubt the English text shall prevail.

For the Government of the Republic of India

Sd/-
P.C. CHUNDER
Minister of Education
Social Welfare and Culture

For the Government of the Republic of Sri Lanka

Sd/-
E.L.B. HURULLE
Minister for Cultural Affairs

APPENDIX IV

CULTURAL COOPERATION AGREEMENT BETWEEN THE GOVERNMENT OF INDIA AND THE GOVERNMENT OF THE PEOPLE'S REPUBLIC OF BANGLADESH

Dacca, 30 December 1972

The Government of the Republic of INDIA

And

The Government of the People's Republic of BANGLADESH

Inspired by the common desire to establish and develop closer cultural relaitons between the two countries in the spirit of the high ideals of the Constitution of the United Nations Educational, Scientific and Cultural Organization; and

DESIROUS OF promoting and developing in every possible manner such relations and understanding between India and Bangladesh especially in the realm of culture, art and education, including academic activity in the fields of science and technology,

HAVE AGREED to conclude the following Cultural Agreement and for that purpose, have nominated their respective plenipotentiaries i.e.:

For the Government of the Republic of India	SHRI S. DUTT High Commissioner for India in Bangladesh
For the Government of the People's Republic of Bangladesh	MR. A.S. NOOR MOHAMMAD Secretary, Ministry of Education Cultural Affairs and Sports

Article I

The Contracting Parties shall endeavour to promote and stimulate cooperation between universities, academies, schools and institutions of higher learning, technical, scientific and art institutions, laboratories and research institutions, libraries and museums. To achieve this objective, the Contracting Parties shall encourage in accordance with their respective internal legislation:

(a) exchange of representatives and delegations in the fields of culture, education, science and arts; and
(b) exchange of cultural, scientific and educational material, translation and exchange of books, periodicals and other scientific, technical and cultural publications, and as far as possible, exchange of archaeological specimens.

Article II

The Contracting Parties shall encourage

(a) reciprocal visits of professors and experts for delivering lectures and conducting special courses, and
(b) reciprocal visits of representatives of literary, scientific, technical, artistic, and journalists' associations and organizations and participation in congresses.

Article III

Each Contracting Party shall grant scholarships to students from the country of the other party for studies in cultural, technical, educational and scientific fields

Article IV

Each Contracting Party shall encourage exhange of scientific, technical and art exhibitions.

Article V

Both Contracting Parties shall encourage dissemination of knowledge of each other's culture through radio, press and similar other channels of mass media.

Article VI

Both Contracting Parties shall encourage exchanges in the field of sports and physical education.

Article VII

Both Contracting Parties shall facilitate exchanges in the following fields:

(a) performances by artistes;
(b) participation in each other's international film festivals; and

(c) films, documentaries, radio and television programmes and recordings and discs and tapes.

Article VIII

Each Contracting Party shall endeavour to ensure that text-books and other educational publications prescribed for educational institutions do not contain any error or misrepresentation of facts about the country of the other Party.

Article IX

The Contracting Parties shall offer their good offices to facilitate the mutual recognition by universities and other edcational authorities in the two countries of the degrees, diplomas and certificates awarded by them in accordance with the laws prevailing in each country.

Article X

Both Contracting Parties shall facilitate and encourage research and study of the allied traditions in the fields of art, literature and history at universities and institutions of higher learning and through establishment of cultural and edcuational centres/institutions, subject to the laws of the respective countires.

Article XI

Both Contracting Parties shall encourage tourist visits by each other's nationals to foster greater understanding and friendship between the two countries.

Article XII

Both Contracting Parties shall encourage the publication of books of each other's country especially books in the fields of science, medicine, law and technology.

Article XIII

For the fulfilment of the objectives of the present Agreement, a Joint Commission will be established, in due course, composed of three representatives of each Contracting Party, and will meet at least once in every two years, alternately in New Delhi and Dacca. To the said Joint Comission may be added representatives from the various Ministers concerned with the implementation of the Agreement of the Contracting Party in whose territory the meeting is to be held, as well as the Diplomatic Mission of the other Party.

The Joint Commission shall be responsible for:

(a) keeping under periodical review the working of the Agreement in the two countries;
(b) advising the two Government on the detailed manner of carrying out the Agreement;
(c) formulating cultural, scientific and educational exchange programmes and reviewing their progress;
(d) recommending to the Party concerned any items of interest to either Party in the fields within the scope of this Agreement; and
(e) generally advising the two Governments as to the manner in which the working of the Agreement may be improved upon.

Article III

The present Agreement shall come into force on the date of exchange of the instruments of ratification, to take place in the city of New Delhi, and shall remain in force until the expiry of six months from the date on which one of the Contracting Parties shall give notice in writing of its intention to terminate the Agreement.

IN WITNESS WHEREOF, the Plenipotentiaries designated earlier have singed the present Agreement and affixed their seals thereon.

DONE in duplicate at Dacca this thirtieth day of December 1972 (Corresponding to the ninth day of Pausa of the Saka year 1894) in Hindi, Bengali and English languages, all the texts being equally authentic.

For the Government of
the Republic of India

Sd/-
S. DUTT
High Commissioner for
India in Bangladesh

For the Government of
the People's Republic of Bangladesh

Sd/-
A.S. NOOR MOHAMMAD
Secretary, Ministry of Education,
Cultural Affairs and Sports

APPENDIX V

AGREEMENT BETWEEN THE GOVERNMENT OF INDIA AND THE GOVERNMENT OF THE ISLAMIC REPUBLIC OF PAKISTAN REGARDING VISA

Islamabad, 14 September 1974

The Government of India

And

The Government of Pakistan

In pursuance of the provisions in the Simla Agreement of July 1972 regarding the extension of travel facilities to nationals of either country desiring to visit the other

HAVE agreed as follows:

1. Nationals of either country visiting the other shall possess a valid passport and a visa for the purpose.
2. The visas will be of the following categories:
   (a) Diplomatic Visa
      (i) A diplomatic visa valid for multiple entries will be issued to the Heads of the Diplomatic and Consular Missions, members of the Mission holding diplomatic or consular rank, their wives and children, and regular Diplomatic Couriers. The period of its validity will ordinarily be one year.
      (ii) A diplomatic visa valid for single entry will be given to high ranking dignitaries. It will also be given to high ranking officials visiting on official business or to attend international conferences and to the members of their families accompanying them. This visa will ordinarily be valid for one month.

   (b) Non-Diplomatic Visa
   A non-diplomatic visa valid for multiple entries will be issued to non-diplomatic members of the Diplomatic or Consular Mission, their wives and children and the personal servants of members of the Mission holding Diplomatic or Consular ranks. The period

of its validity will ordinarily be one year. It will be valid for stay at the place of assignment which will be specified and shall also be valid for journeys performed while accompanying a holder of a diplomatic visa.

(c) Official Visa

An official visa valid for single entry will be issued to officials not entitled to diplomatic or non-diplomatic visa of either country visiting the other on official business including participation in international conferences. This visa will ordinarily be valid for one month and for specified places.

(d) Visitor Visa

(i) A visitor visa will be issued to persons visiting the other country to meet relatives or friends, for business or any other legitimate purpose. This visa shall be for single entry and valid for a period not exceeding three months. However, the visa may be issued for a longer period not exceeding one year if owing to the nature of work or businesses a prolonged stay is necessary.

(ii) Places to be visited shall be specified in the visa.

(e) Transit Visa

Transit visa valid for stay in the city/port of entry for 72 hours will be issued to persons travelling by air or sea and procedding to another country through Pakistan/India. No visa will be required for a passenger directly transiting through an airport/seaport, but his stay shall be confined to the area in the airport/seaport set apart for international transit passengers.

GENERAL PROVISIONS

3. If a visa is not availed of within three months of the date of its issue, it shall stand cancelled. The period of validity of a visa for stay shall count from the date of entry.

4. For the nationals of either country going to/coming from the other country. These checkposts shall be specified on the visas.

(a) By Air: Karachi/Lahore/Islamabad (Pakistan) and Bombay/Delhi/Amritsar (India)

(b) By Sea: Karachi (Pakistan) and Bombay (India)

(c) By Land: Wagha/Attari and Khokrapar/Munabao border checkposts.

5. Registration

Holders of visitor and transit visa shall be required to register themselves at the checkposts of entry and shall, within 24 hours of their reaching in the specified place of stay, report their arrival in writing to the prescribed authority or the nearest police station. They shall also make a similar report 24 hours prior to their intended departure from the place of stay.

6. Seaman

   A seaman visiting a port as a member of the crew of a ship need not hold a Passport or a Visa. He may be issued a Landing Permit valid for the port of entry for a period not exceeding 24 hours, provided he deposits his Continuous Discharge Certificate (nullie) with the Immigration authorities.

7. Fee

   A fee of Rupees five Pakistani/Indian will be payable for the issuance or extension of visitor or transit Visas.

8. This Agreement supercedes all previous Agreements on the subject.

SIGNED at Islamabad on September 14, 1974.

For the Government of India	For the Government of Pakistan
Sd/-	Sd/-
KEWAL SINGH	AGHA SHAHI
Foreign Secretary	Foreign Secretary
Government of India	Government of Pakistan

People-to-People Contact in South Asia, Scope and Constraints

SHAHID KARDAR

Introduction

The present level of contact and degree of interaction between the people of South Asia, and particularly between the citizens of Pakistan and India, is rather low. The variety of political, perceptual and economic obstacles to people-to-people contact are aggravated by the restrictions imposed on free travel by many countries in the region through their administrative procedures and mechanisms.

It is due to this lack of people-to-people contact that the efforts for regional cooperation have not borne fruit. Almost every SAARC summit has reiterated the need for boosting intra-region travel generally by removing various constraints but little has been achieved. The main hurdle to the fruition of the dream associated with people-to-people contact is the strained relations between Pakistan and India.

Objectives of The Study

The principle that mutual benefits arise from a freer flow of information, goods and services between countries is well established and does not require justification. In South Asia, this greater interaction between the people of the region will also be particularly helpful in improving an understanding of each other's concerns and perceptions and thereby contribute to a reduction in tensions between governments. The need to look into the scope of, and constraints to, people-to-people contact in the SAARC region provides the basis for this collaborative study. This part of the study examines the impediments to travel within the region, with special emphasis on the Indo-Pakistan dimension.

The objective of the study is to examine the following broad categories of factors that restrict a more productive people-to-people contact:

(*a*) The gaps and discrepancies between the existing legal, policy and other provisions and their implementation.

(*b*) The perceptual and political constraints including, among others, the lack of continuous support for the intensification of regional trade and cooperation, the environment of hostility, and the threat to national security and survival as portrayed by the more vocal groups in society.

Scope of The Study

The study reviews the existing literature and current laws, procedures and regulations. In the process, a sample of senior officials in the Ministry of Interior at the Federal level and in the Home Department in the Provincial Government of Punjab were interviewed. To ascertain the difficulties and constraints faced by key economic players in obtaining information and conducting trade, the study also interviewed key officials of the two major Chambers of Commerce in the country, Karachi and Lahore, the SAARC Chamber of Commerce and Industry and key individuals in a sample of non-governmental organisations actively pursuing inter-regional dialogue and sharing information on matters of mutual concern.

It reviews the objectives underlying the restrictions placed on the movement of people, the methods adopted to achieve these objectives, the pressure building up against such restrictions because of private and non-governmental initiatives, the pressures of globalisation and international arrangements (like the WTO) and how these factors are expected to influence the pattern and quality of intra-regional cooperation.

While examining the restrictions faced on account of government policies and procedures, the study also highlights the failure in implementing the SAARC Visa Exemption Scheme in extending its scope beyond its currently limited and highly restricted application.

Finally, the study contains a succinct assessment of the infrastructural constraints in the movement of people—examines the issues of access and the quality of communication and transportation facilities.

Constraints Relating to People-to-People Contact

For advocates of regional cooperation, people-to-people contact is a prerequisite for accelerating the process of regional cooperation. However, people-to-people contact is hindered by a variety of cumbersome entry and travel procedures that restrict movement across borders even for the purposes of trade and business. These controls are a major reason for the slow progress in economic cooperation among the countries in the region. The tension between India and Pakistan, because of decades of strained relations and three wars, overshadows all other regional issues and makes progress on the agenda of SAARC difficult. India's predominance in the region also induces anxieties amongst its smaller neighbours.

The host of administrative mechanisms and procedural and political impediments to the freer movement of people (especially between Pakistan and India) in the region, are reinforced, if not compounded, by the fears and apprehensions anchored in the social and political psyche—made worse by the security and threat perceptions built up by years of indoctrination through the media on one hand and, on the other hand, by official sanction through distorted history curricula taught in schools.

The study, therefore, deals with the issue at three levels—perceptual, legislative and procedural. The first, and most crucial factor, concerns the wide gulf in perceptions of the people of different countries regarding each other, on the basis of which the edifice of the state structure has been built through the promotion of state ideologies. The difficulty of overcoming the negative and retarding aspects of these perceptions has been complicated by the strange political circumstances that led to the partition of the subcontinent.

The animosity has, over the years, been reinforced by subsequent institutional and political developments. This aspect of the issue has been discussed at some length merely to highlight the key constraint to enhanced people-to-people contact, which cannot be addressed by the recommendations contained in a report dealing with travel related issues. The necessary change required for a meaningful resolution of issues relating to people-to-people contact can only come through a painstakingly consistent demonstration of political will and determination to resolve the long-standing issues. Moreover, such efforts will have to be accompanied by interim measures to gradually lower the level of tension.

At the second level, the existing laws and procedures that govern or regulate the entry, exit and movement of travellers from SAARC countries within Pakistan were reviewed and analysed. It seems that administrative procedures have been designed to discourage the travel of South Asians within their own region. The long queues and crowds at the gates of the High Commissions of India and Pakistan reflect the eagerness of people to travel but only a fraction are able to obtain the necessary visas. Despite the stringency of existing regulations, there is room for officials to adopt a sympathetic attitude and to raise their level of efficiency. This in itself could effect considerable improvements in the present status. Hypothetically, if the perceptual constraints were to be removed, existing legislation and rules could be easily modified. At times some relaxation has been witnessed, largely because of the personal initiative of a foreign minister or as a consequence of a liberal stance temporarily assumed by a government. The recommendations in this regard could become effective if there is sufficient public pressure on the respective administrations.

At the procedural level, some changes and reforms have been introduced as a result of the efforts of the organisation for regional cooperation in South Asia, SAARC. The foundations have been laid, through various resolutions and agreements under SAARC, which await sincere implementation. Public pressure, supported by the efforts of non-governmental organisations, can play an instrumental role in getting respective governments to implement speedily the broad decisions reached under the aegis of SAARC. To this end the study recommends the speedy implementation of the recommendations of SAARC for which some ground has already been broken and the implementation of which is, therefore, likely to face least resistance. Other suggestions of the study focus on ways to change official attitudes by breaking the moulds created by the outmoded notions of the bureaucratic structures of both Pakistan and India.

THE PERCEPTUAL CONSTRAINTS

The nature of Indo-Pakistan relations is the main obstacle to people-to-people contact in South Asia. The state of tension and rivalry between these two countries has not only curbed travel but is also responsible for the poor people-to-people contact among the peoples of other countries in South Asia. For instance, it is a challenging task for Nepal, Bangladesh and Sri Lanka to develop close relations with Pakistan through economic, social and cultural interaction because such efforts would be construed in India as alliances with India's enemy. Similarly, the Pakistani establishment, unhappy with an improvement in India's relationship with its other neighbours, would like to restrict visitors from these countries on the plea that Indians might infiltrate Pakistan posing as Bangladeshis, Sri Lankans or Nepalis. At first sight these perceptions may be viewed as overstating the case because there are no special economic, social and cultural linkages between Pakistan, Nepal and Sri Lanka. By ignoring the verities of geography, such perceptions only serve to inhibit linkages. However, India's recent attempts to improve its economic relationships with its other neighbours were viewed with concern by the Pakistan government. It regarded such liberal efforts as a deliberate Indian move to isolate Pakistan which also ran contrary to the multilateral spirit of SAARC.

Perceptions rooted in history are the more intractable hurdles in the way of a meaningful resolution of people-to-people contact related issues. Animosities predate the Independence of Pakistan and India in 1947 and existed in the period under the colonial occupation.[1] The carnage and mayhem during the large scale migration of people across the dividing lines established in 1947 concretised the animosity. This experience in particular rendered it difficult for the people of the two nations to develop friendly relations. Still worse, many issues like the status of Junagarh, Hyderabad, Jammu and Kashmir, and distribution of assets remained unsettled. These provided enough fuel to sustain the fires of enmity. Pakistan and India thus got locked into their hostile postures, and perceptions and prejudices got frozen in time vitiating the climate for peace. The following examples illustrate the nature of this problem:

- The commonly held Pakistani perception about Indians is that they cannot be trusted. They are viewed as devious. Only Pakistanis truly understand the 'Hindu mind'.
- The Indians have never accepted the existence of Pakistan. They are constantly scheming to destabilise Pakistan, its break-up being their primary goal. India was responsible for the creation of Bangladesh and its ultimate desire is to merge Pakistan with India.
- The distribution of territory and assets at the time of partition was not fair by Pakistan. Muslims got a moth-eaten Pakistan, while India usurped the state of Jammu and Kashmir which should have become a part of Pakistan.
- Official Indian declarations on secularism are viewed as a poor attempt to appease and co-opt the Muslims in India, whereas, in reality, India is not secular. It is a Hindu state, extremely antagonistic towards Islam.
- The continuing expansion of the Indian defence establishment despite its superior military strength, the target being Pakistan. The principal duty of a Pakistani is to provide the resources required to augment and strengthen the country's defence capabilities to enable the armed forces to meet any threat from a much larger enemy.

[1] As a deliberate policy measure, the British also aggravated these tensions.

The Indian perceptions about Pakistan are summarised below:

- Pakistanis have aggressive designs against India since they cannot even manage their own internal affairs.
- Pakistanis lack democratic culture. The authoritarian structure and the continued role of the military as a power broker are the main obstacles to peace.
- Pakistan has been supporting insurgency in India—be it Punjab, the north-eastern states or Kashmir—through money, men and materials. Kashmir is an integral part of India. The uprising in the valley is India's internal affair. Its secularism and democracy has the ability to overcome such irritants.
- Pakistan has not made concerted efforts to promote regional interests. It has played the role of an agent of imperialist and western powers.
- Islamic fundamentalism is the new danger emanating from Pakistan.

These perceptual differences, having become stuck in a groove, are stoutly reflected in the policy-making processes, the existing rules and their implementation. These stereotyped concepts are, as described earlier, reinforced as well as maintained through the media and the curricula of schools and colleges. As a consequence, efforts to promote people-to-people contact are strongly undermined and even recommendations for procedural changes are resisted.

Even after years the ruling elites still appear to be unwilling to move out of these set moulds. At the same time, many believe that present anxieties, and the bulk of the existing political problems, have been magnified by certain influential groups on both sides of the border in their own interests—they thrive on the existence of tensions, the maintenance of an environment of distrust, and a heightened sense of insecurity. Special interest groups, in particular the intelligence agencies on both sides, play a negative role in the establishment of détente because of the high stakes—their importance in the domestic decision-making processes and, as a resultant better access to resources and the political leadership—they hold on to such an adversarial relationship.

The compulsions of domestic politics, particularly for weak political leaderships ruling through coalition governments or without large-scale public support, also make it difficult to proceed with the level of determination required to nullify the dragging effects of the experiences of the past. The fear of attracting adverse domestic public opinion and the opposition of the hardline, 'fundamentalist', groups on both sides renders them unable to make the concessions necessary for creating the environment conducive for peace. There is anxiety that the opposition might be able to channelise and translate public opprobrium to improvement in bilateral relations into election victories.

OBSTACLES CREATED BY LEGISLATION AND ADMINISTRATIVE PROCEDURES

Before examining the legislative and procedural constraints for people-to-people contact it would be pertinent to identify the agencies mandated to devise policies concerning the entry and exit of foreign nationals and examine the rules pertaining to the entry into, and movement within, Pakistan of the citizens of SAARC countries.

Policy-making

The rules relating to the processing of visa applications and the type and scope of discretionary powers devolved to the heads of Pakistani missions are formulated by the Ministry of Interior. All policy-making in this regard is essentially the prerogative of this Ministry. These policies and decisions are then implemented by the Foreign Office, Ministry of Foreign Affairs.

The Ministry of Foreign Affairs has only an advisory role in this regard. Visa Officers belong to the Ministry of Interior. Although the Ambassadors/High Commissioners have some discretionary powers, and can overrule the decisions of personnel granting visas, this would be an exception rather than the norm.

Presently, Pakistani embassies in 43 countries (see Appendix I for complete list of countries) enjoy full powers to issue visas to businessmen and most other categories of travellers (excluding journalists) and are not required to refer to the Ministry of Interior or the Home Department of the relevant Provincial Government.

Governing Legislation and Accompanying Rules

The Foreigners Act, 1946, The Pakistan Control of Entry Act, 1952, and The Registration of Foreigners Act, 1939, as amended from time to time, are the governing legislation pertaining to the entry of foreigners into Pakistan, their movement and residence within, and eventual exit from, the country. Rules and orders, which elaborate upon the provisions of such legislation, are developed by the Federal Government.

For instance, Section 3 of the Foreigners Act empowers the Federal Government to issue orders or make rules either of general nature or those with respect to any class of, or any particular foreigner, for prohibiting, regulating or restricting their entry into, exit from, and continued presence in, Pakistan.

Exercising the powers conferred by Section 3 of this Act, the Government of Pakistan issued the Enemy Foreigners Order, 1965, which places restrictions on the movement of foreigners possessing the nationality of a state at war with Pakistan.

However, Rule 11 of the Registration of Foreigners Rules, 1966, drawn under Section 3 of the Foreigners Act, requires an Indian citizen holding a visa category other than A, C and E (the last mentioned applies to transport workers) to:

(*a*) report absence from his registered address for seven days or more to the Registration Officer of the district of his registered address and provide his current address; or

(*b*) report, within 24 hours of his arrival, his presence to the Registration Officer of the district in which he is currently residing, if he has already stayed, or intends to stay, seven days or more in that district.

The Pakistan Control of Entry Act, 1952, which controls the entry of Indian citizens into Pakistan, is a piece of legislation which was essentially drafted to restrict the migration of Indians into

Pakistan. The currency of its application is derived from Section 8 which empowers the Federal Government to make rules on the types of visas which may be granted, and the conditions and restrictions which may be imposed on a traveller, such as the fixing and notification of check-posts and routes and the procedure for registration and reporting to police required under the rules for certain categories of visa holders.

The free movement of nationals of other countries is regulated under the administrative rules, notifications and orders referred to above. In other words, Indians are treated separately under laws for visa issuance under the operation of executive instruction and the difficulties that travellers from India to Pakistan have to grapple with do not arise because of any discriminatory legislation but because of the procedures formulated under its subsections. The restrictions in existing procedures also reflect the baneful influences of reciprocity and the inevitable reaction to any action by the other country.

The system of granting visas, the bilateral agreements in this regard, the administrative set-up/style of the High Commissions or Embassies of SAARC countries, etc., are both planned and implemented in a manner that discourages the flow of intra-regional visitors, although personal initiatives (for example those of a foreign minister) or a more liberal policy in specific areas at specific time periods of a particular government do make a difference. A recent example in support of this statement are the steps taken by the Indian Ministry of External Affairs for a more relaxed policy of granting visas to Pakistani visitors. Nevertheless, no change in policy, rules or their implementation thereof, has taken place formally.

These obstacles are the structural impediments to people-to-people contact among the SAARC countries. But the situation gets worse when these are superimposed by the perceptual predilections of the implementing officials, derived both from official policy/procedures as interpreted by them and peer group and societal pressure. However, even if rules are tough, their application in a liberal, sympathetic and efficient manner, can improve the situation significantly.

PROBLEMS IN IMPLEMENTING SAARC PROPOSALS

Although modest steps have been proposed and taken during the last decade to nurture cooperation in the region, even these could not be implemented fully because of the disheartening situation of bilateral relations between Pakistan and India. Therefore, little has been built on the foundations laid initially. Nevertheless, gradual improvements in bilateral relations are discernible in people-to-people contact. This section discusses the relevant developments focusing on the weak implementation of these decisions.

- As early as December 1985, in the Dhaka declaration, the SAARC Heads of States emphasized that 'strengthening of regional cooperation in South Asia required greater involvement of their people. They agreed to increase interaction and further promote people-to-people contact at various levels among their countries (Article 8).' This was again mentioned in Article 7 of the Bangalore declaration in November 1987 and was reiterated at all subsequent summits. In April 1993, at the Seventh SAARC Summit in Dhaka, the Heads of States 'noted that the formulation of guidelines and procedures for extending recognitions to regional apex bodies would facilitate participation of these bodies in promoting regional cooperation at the people-to-people level'. And during the next Summit they 'noted with satisfaction that such interaction has (had) been taking place'.
- SAARC claims that it has promoted people-to-people contact in the region through the following initiatives:

  (i) SAARC Audio-Visual Exchange Programme
  (ii) SAARC Documentation Centre
  (iii) SAARC Scheme for Promotion of Organised Tourism
  (iv) SAARC Chairs, Fellowships and Scholarship Scheme
  (v) SAARC Youth Volunteers Programme
  (vi) SAARC Visa Exemption Scheme (VES)
  (vii) South Asian Festivals
  (viii) Non-governmental Organisations, such as: Association of SAARC Speakers and Parliamentarians; SAARC Chamber of Commerce and Industry; SAARC Law; and recently a body on SAARC Labour.

However, except the Visa Exemption Scheme or NGO activity other initiatives have had little impact on the situation. Nevertheless, when compared with the past situation, there has been an improvement. The number of travellers other than those in the category of divided families has increased.[2] The level and quality of cooperation among NGOs has grown appreciably and there is greater public awareness of the initiatives that have been taken by citizen groups to improve Indo-Pakistan relations.

The difficulties in implementing proposals under SAARC provide an explanation of the failure to make any meaningful headway in operationalising specifically drafted, general and, wholesome provisions for promoting people-to-people contact. For example, in the Simla Agreement the attempt to normalise relations between India and Pakistan accepted the need to 'promote travel facilities, trade and cooperation in economic and other fields', etc.

Procedures for Visas

The procedures governing the issuance of visas are derived from bilateral agreements between two countries. Different categories of visas and the permissible number of visas in each category, the number of visa officers and related staff are matters decided on a reciprocal basis although room exists for relaxing visa policies. Whereas the number of discretionary visas which can be issued is limited by the agreements, it lies within the discretion of a High Commissioner to accommodate any visa category under his quota. However, if one country initiates or maintains a liberal policy and opens up travel to nationals of another country it is not binding on the latter country to reciprocate these initiatives. Hence, although a unilateral liberalisation of visa restrictions is possible, it is likely to

[2] Although official statistics are not available, there is anecdotal evidence, also supported by the higher number and frequency of flights, that the number of travellers from Pakistan's Punjab has increased. However, following the closure of the Consulates in Mumbai and Karachi the net increase in the number of travellers may well have been nominal even if it has not actually declined.

be short-lived if it is not reciprocated. In fact, the country reluctant to reciprocate would discourage its nationals from visiting the other country. For instance, the Pakistan Government, by making exit procedures more stringent and cumbersome, could actually nullify the advantages theoretically made available to Pakistanis from the liberalisation undertaken by other countries in South Asia.

Travellers to Pakistan are categorised according to reasons of their travel. These reasons could be for business purposes, to attend a conference/seminar, to visit spouse or relatives, journalistic assignments, pilgrimage, to attend a meeting or a function of any kind (administrative, educational, social, cultural, sports, religious, etc.), and to work. Most of the requirements that foreign nationals travelling to Pakistan have to fulfil are not applied selectively to those from the South Asia region; they are encountered by nationals of other countries as well.

Once the purpose of travel has been established four different methods are adopted in issuing visas. The first type covers visas processed under the aegis of a pre-verification system; then there are processed visas; the next category of visas are issued by Pakistani Missions abroad (generally covered by the discretionary quota[3]); and finally, visas issued under the SAARC Visa Exemption Scheme.

Visas for business purpose, to attend conferences and meet spouses can be classified as process visas, since the process starts either from the parent country or the host country. And at the time an application for a visa is filed, the necessary approval has already reached the concerned High Commission/Embassy. Visas for journalists or members of divided families pass through a pre-verification system. Permission—a no objection certificate (NOC)—for a visiting journalist has to be sent by the Ministry of Information

[3] Reliable statistics on the volume of travel between Pakistan and India or other SAARC countries are hard to obtain. None the less, the Pakistani High Commissions in Bangladesh, Sri Lanka or India have a discretionary quota enabling them to issue between 300 to 400 visas per month.

to the Ministry of Interior giving specific approval for a visa. In the same way, applications for official visas traverse the departmental paths. For private visits to meet relatives the verification has to be carried out by the Special Branch in the Police Department of the concerned province and then permission is sent from the Ministry of Interior, Federal Government, to the concerned consulate/embassy/high commission to grant of a visa.

Although the most liberal treatment is accorded to business travellers,[4] in most cases the visiting businessman has to provide, as evidence of his bona fides, an invitation from a business contact in Pakistan.

In the case of seminars arranged by a public sector agency, those attending the conference are required to furnish the invitation of the conference organisers, while the sponsoring ministry/authority/agency applies to the Directorate of the Ministry of External Affairs dealing with the country whose nationals are being invited. The political clearance, to enable such visitors to participate in the conference, is given by the Ministry of Foreign Affairs, subject to the final approval of the Ministry of Interior, or of the authority/officer to whom powers to accord such a permission have been devolved by the Ministry of Interior.

Pakistani academics or academics from other countries seeking visas to enter Pakistan have to submit their applications to the Ministry of Interior or the Home Department through the Ministry or Department of Education respectively.

The application of a journalist wishing to visit Pakistan has to be specifically approved by the External Publicity Wing of the Ministry of Information.[5] This requirement exists because governments in Pakistan have traditionally been highly sensitive to their image as portrayed in the international media. Conscious of the implications of any negative publicity, visits of foreign journalists are not actively encouraged.

[4] Even Indian businessmen can be issued one-year visas which entitle them to three entries.

[5] The External Publicity Wing is also responsible for arranging interviews with the Prime Minister or the President, if the journalist planning a visit were to make such a request.

The Visa Exemption Scheme

The Visa Exemption Scheme (VES) was initiated in 1988; it became operational from 1 March 1992 and so far 1,600 visas have been issued under it. Currently, persons entitled to the scheme are judges of the supreme court, members of the national parliaments, heads of national academic institutions, foreign/permanent secretaries dealing with foreign affairs, SAARC Secretary General and Directors of the SAARC Secretariat, Presidents of national Chambers of Commerce and Industry and their accompanying spouses and dependent children below 18 years of age. Special visa exemption stickers produced under the auspices of the SAARC Secretariat are available with the Foreign Office or the SAARC Secretariat. These are meant to be pasted on the traveller's passport.

Practically all SAARC summits have reiterated the commitment to promote travel facilities and extend the net of the VES beyond members of each others legislature, senior government officials and heads of the respective national Chambers of Commerce and Industry and to encourage NGOs and other office-bearers of the local Chambers of Commerce. Progress, however, has been slow and substantive efforts to achieve the cherished goals have not made much headway. For instance, the Pakistan government has not yet agreed to the proposal that the Vice-Presidents of the Chambers of Commerce and Industry should also qualify under the VES. Their counter proposal is that the scheme's ambit should be extended to cover senior officials of the Immigration Department.

Visitors from SAARC Countries other than India

Citizens of some countries within the SAARC region such as Bangladesh and Sri Lanka, excluding India, visiting their relatives are able to establish their bona fides with the Pakistani mission and obtain a visa from the discretionary quota held by the heads of missions. Those unable to satisfy the embassy about their credentials have to be cleared by the pre-verification system. Visa applications not entertained by the head of mission, using the discretionary quota held by him, are faxed, or sent through diplomatic bag, to the Ministry of Foreign Affairs and the Ministry of Interior or to any authority to whom powers have been delegated by the Ministry of Interior.

Nationals of Nepal and Maldives are not required to apply for a visa provided their stay in Pakistan does not exceed one month. This provision for a one-month visa exemption is not widely known and travellers from Nepal and Maldives generally obtain visas before undertaking the visit.

Travellers from Sri Lanka, Bangladesh and Bhutan are not granted a visa at the discretion of the head of the respective High Commission/Embassy. They have to await the specific permission of the respective provincial government in whose jurisdiction their destination falls.

Nationals of Bangladesh are required to report either at the point of entry or at the city where they plan to spend most of their time in Pakistan. On leaving the city, they are again required to report to the police and obtain permission to exit; they have to inform the police the period within which they will exit from Pakistan, generally not exceeding a week from the date of informing the police about their intention to leave the country. During this period, the Bangladeshi national can visit any part of Pakistan and exit the country from any port.

The restrictions on the free entry and movement of Bangladeshi nationals stem from three exaggerated, although not entirely misplaced, fears:

(*a*) Those entering Pakistan may be Biharis (who perceive themselves as Pakistanis) who do not wish to remain in Bangladesh and have decided to settle in Pakistan like many other Biharis who came to Pakistan before them.

(*b*) Some travellers from less affluent backgrounds may stay back in Pakistan to work as domestic servants without valid work permits.

(*c*) Indian intelligence agents may infiltrate Pakistani territory posing as Bangladeshi nationals. Hence, entry has to be restricted in the interest of public safety.

In the case of Sri Lanka as well (*b*) and (*c*) have been

mentioned as factors hindering the freer travel and movement of Sri Lankan nationals to Pakistan.

Pakistan lacks the administrative apparatus (in terms of number of personnel) and related infrastructure (including an information base, mobility for personnel) to conduct a proper and speedy verification of an application prior to the issue of a visa.[6] Hence, it can take anything from between two to four months from the time that the application is filed to the actual receipt of the permission from the Pakistan government to enable the traveller to undertake the journey.

The Ministry of Interior, however, insists that, by and large, all genuine travellers from SAARC countries (other than India) are granted permission by the Pakistani Embassy/High Commission. Others, although inconvenienced by the circuitous and cumbersome process, get the necessary approval from the Home Department or the Ministries of Interior, Information or Education. Officials in the Ministry claim that they are not aware of any serious complaints registered by nationals of Bangladesh about the treatment meted out to travellers who are able to furnish adequate proof of their identity.

Travellers from India

Indian travellers to Pakistan, particularly those engaged in non-official dialogues, complain about the harassment, and to some extent intimidation, that they have to face at the hands of the intelligence agencies. The harassment suffered by them due to overt and deliberately humiliating surveillance methods runs contrary to the spirit and intent of SAARC efforts to promote freer travel. By raising suspicions, it spoils the environment for extending the ambit of, and the nature of participation in, dialogue. In contravention of the agreed Code of Conduct, it is also common for visitors to the Indian High Commission to be questioned by policemen in plain clothes stationed outside the High Commission premises. The

[6] The formidable nature of the task becomes more understandable considerating the general problem of bureaucratic attitudes towards the processing of applications, even by their own nationals, let alone aliens.

harassment of diplomatic personnel and their families is now almost routine; periodic expulsions also contribute to the hardening of attitudes.

Processing an application is largely on the basis of guidelines rather than specific legislation. There is also no mechanism for enquiring into the reasons for rejection of an application. In both Pakistan and India, visa seekers are generally accorded rough treatment. Visas, in general, are city specific and for a short period of seven to fifteen days duration. Moreover, visitors have to report to the police at the time of entry, exit and during the stay; a visa exempting a traveller from reporting to the police is considered a privilege. In addition, the attitude of the immigration officers and customs personnel at the port of entry/exit if not positively discouraging, is not cordial.

In Prime Minister I.K. Gujral's tenure, there appears to be some change in the attitude of the Indian High Commission in Pakistan. This may be transient. Being the personal initiative of the then Indian External Affairs Minister (now Prime Minister), it has not yet been declared a policy change. In any case, the provisions are clearly inadequate. Long queues, coupons, lucky draws and stringent processing of visas are natural outcomes which seriously undermine the people-to-people interaction in the region. Anecdotal evidence, however, suggests that the number of visas granted by the Indian High Commission on a working day is significantly larger than the number of visas issued by the Pakistan High Commission. Earlier, 30 to 40 lucky draws were held per working day for the applicants falling in the category of relatives. This number appears to have been increased in 1997.

However, the Pakistani Foreign Office dismisses the Indian claim that more visa applications for travel were processed and substantially more people visited India as a result of the liberalisation introduced under the guidance and open door policy of Mr. Gujral. Officials in the Foreign Office maintain that the Indians are heavy on rhetoric, which is appropriately backed by well-orchestrated media propaganda. They contend that in practical terms the change was neither substantial nor tangible, and follow-up actions were poor in comparison with the widely publicised intentions. Their contention is that even the anecdotal evidence in support of this declaration is rather weak, since Pakistanis continue to have difficulty in getting visas even to participate in activities organised under the auspices of SAARC.

LACK OF INFRASTRUCTURE AND PREVALENCE OF OTHER TRAVEL RELATED CONSTRAINTS

Adequate and cheap modes of travel are required to improve the interaction between the ordinary citizens of Pakistan and India. Presently, however, there is only one train *Samjhauta Express* between India and Pakistan, which runs twice a week between Lahore and Delhi. As Pakistani/Indians are generally not allowed to cross Attari/Wagah border by road, there is no bus service connecting Lahore and Amritsar or Lahore and Delhi. The Indian/Pakistani visitors have to be laboriously packed in the slow moving *Samjhauta* train and can only disembark/embark at Lahore or Delhi.

Even for those who can afford to travel by air, there is an inadequate number of flights and connections. Very few cities are connected to each other directly and where they are, these are infrequent. Even capital cities of South Asia are not directly connected to each other, particularly Islamabad and transit visas are difficult to obtain.

Similarly, there is a severely restricted number of valid entry/exit points between SAARC countries. All these factors dampen the urge to travel among the SAARC countries, particularly between Pakistan and India.

In addition, there are other irritants by way of the restrictions on foreign currency and printed material that travellers can carry with them. Furthermore, these rules are implemented in such a naïve fashion that no significant purpose appears to be served and ordinary travellers feel discouraged and harassed.

CONSTRAINTS TO ECONOMIC COOPERATION

Although there are repeated exhortations from all sides on the need to intensify efforts to strengthen economic cooperation under the auspices of the SAARC Preferential Trading Agreement (SAPTA), the political commitment to the development of meaningful economic and trade relations continues to be weak, as reflected in the modest coverage of tradable products under SAPTA.

A key constraint to a more open economic environment is the fear of intensified competition that will be encountered by economic agents in different sectors and sub-sectors of the economy as a result of greater penetration by producers of other countries once they are given more space. And if these fears can feed upon perceptions of threat to the survival of a key sector of the economy because of the potential strength of one economy to bring to its knees the active sector/sub-sector of the other economy, then the economic impediments can further discourage trade and, consequently, more open people-to-people contact.

There is also a perceived threat to jobs and other economic opportunities as a result of a freer flow of cheap labour. Although these fears are highly exaggerated, the examples generally quoted in support of actions restricting the freer movement by people include the cases of 'Sri Lankan maids' and 'Bangladeshi cooks'.

Nevertheless, there are several advantages to expanding trade between Pakistan and India. The rest of this section discusses these and other trade related aspects in detail.

Advantages of Trade with India

On the surface, the two economies may seem to be in competition with each other. In view of the lack of adequate information the formulation of such a view is understandable. As there is limited economic contact between the two countries greater emphasis is being laid on the problems likely to be encountered because of the differences in tariff structures.

However, advantages of geography—cheaper transportation costs—and trade complementarity in goods in which each country has a comparative advantage, are overwhelming. Proximity and a similarity of culture and consumption patterns should provide both trade opportunities and a freer flow of information and ideas. There is also some evidence of complementarity in trading activities. There are sub-sectors in agriculture and industry in which trade and cooperation between the two can be mutually beneficial.

For instance, the less affluent Pakistani consumer would benefit from the import of cheaper medicines from India, less expensive Indian cotton/synthetic cloth, while the more privileged consumer will get access to Indian silk products, shawls, saris, etc. Not only will there be more varieties of products available, but prices will also fall with a smoother flow of traded goods. Furthermore, bicycles, scooters, motorcycles and motor vehicles up to 1000 cc manufactured in India are half the price of those produced in Pakistan. Consumers would benefit if Pakistan lowers its duty rates on such items. At the same time Pakistani producers of automotive plastic parts would be well placed to improve capacity utilisation by exploiting the advantages accruing from economies of scale.

The proximity of markets will not only render it unnecessary for industry to carry high levels of inventory, thereby reducing costs of operations, but the opening up of trade with India will also have a salutary effect on prices. By depressing inflation rates it will also ease the inflationary burden on hapless consumers on both sides of the border.

Cooperation in the agricultural sector could be particularly beneficial to Pakistani farmers. They would benefit from the gains made by India in new seed, irrigation and mechanical technologies and its successes in the development of high yield varieties of crops. India has higher yields for all major crops except cotton, in which Pakistan's yield is almost twice that of India's. India has an advantage in rice, maize and grains. Pakistan's basmati rice, citrus fruits and mangoes should have a demand in India, while Indian vegetables, fruits and perishables could be sold in Pakistan. With better access to Indian research and extension services, seeds and agricultural implements, Pakistan, with its large irrigation network, could make major gains.

Indian industries producing machine tools and capital goods are regarded as more developed and efficient than their Pakistani counterparts. Therefore, access to cheaper capital goods should, by reducing the cost of investment, also improve the productivity and efficiency of Pakistani industry. However, due to prevailing political tensions and the high degree of mistrust between the two countries, Pakistani industrialists may be reluctant to purchase plant and equipment from India even if trade is opened up. This hesitation is understandable in view of the perceived operational problems that would have to be faced by potential buyers of machinery in respect of access to spare parts and components in the event of heightened friction.

Recent estimates suggest that the main illegal imports from India are betel leaves, tea, nuts, spices, tyres and tubes, to the value of around US $250 million per annum. If trade in these goods were to flow through official channels the additional customs related revenues would range between Rs. 2.0 to 2.5 billion (US $60 million). Consumers will also benefit from the legalisation of trade with the reduction in the high margins included in prices as a result of smuggling.

Fears of Trade with India

The fear of the Pakistani manufacturing sector that it would be swamped and rendered uncompetitive by Indian industry is highly exaggerated. The average Pakistani consumer has tended to be more quality conscious than the consumer in India. Hence, Pakistani industry has, for a long time, had to compete against both smuggled goods and official imports under the highly generous baggage schemes (for resident and overseas Pakistani travelling or returning to Pakistan). Industry has, therefore, learnt to survive against the heavy competition that it has had to face on account of liberal government policies and rather porous national borders.

The light engineering sector could become a casualty unless Pakistani producers are provided a level playing field through a rationalisation of the tariff structure to enable them to compete effectively with Indian products.

The tariff regime (comprising both tariff and non-tariff barriers) in India continues to be restrictive. Also, India's policies and practices, involving concessional financial assistance, subsidies, tax exemption and R&D funding to industries may be in conflict with the provisions of the GATT agreement. Dumping by Indian producers of bicycles, motorcycles, garments, leather goods, polyester yarn, some textile machinery, calculators, air conditioners, etc., is, therefore, feared. These factors are currently hindering the exchange of agreed lists of commodities for zero/reduced tariffs under SAPTA.

A major concern that Pakistan will have to guard against could be predatory trade practices that India, because of its size, could afford to indulge in. The Indian government could take a conscious decision to help a segment of the Indian manufacturing sector destroy Pakistan's capability in that sector, e.g. textiles, through dumping and discriminatory tariffs. To avert such an eventuality Pakistan will have to considerably strengthen its regulatory infrastructure to handle issues of dumping and counter valuing duties.

The nature, level and products in which trade between the two countries may eventually take place will essentially depend upon the availability of information on production facilities and technologies and the ease with which people in general, and manufacturers and traders in particular, can travel from their home country to the other. The example of South East Asia shows that a lot of trade in the area is intra-regional, suggesting that countries in a region grow together and that no one country in a depressed region can grow rapidly in isolation. In other words, if trade between the two countries is to be promoted their governments will have to play a much more positive role. The viability of the process will depend upon a continuing political commitment in support of an expanded degree of trade.

Pressures of Globalisation

As mentioned earlier, other pressures to open up borders are also mounting, largely owing to increasing economic globalisation and the international agreements (like the WTO) signed by Pakistan. As a member of the WTO, Pakistan is under an obligation to adopt a non-discriminatory approach in its trade with all countries. This non-discriminatory treatment has to be unconditional and Pakistan has no choice in this matter. In its trading transactions, and in matters concerning the grant of access to its markets, Pakistan has to observe the rules of the WTO and treat all WTO members equally, without prejudice.

Pakistan has so far resisted Indian demands for a MFN status under the WTO on the plea that India employs non-tariff trade barriers and that the liberal subsidies it has given to its exports could damage Pakistani industry irreparably. However, Pakistan's protests will almost certainly be rejected by the WTO unless it can furnish concrete evidence in support of its contention. Under WTO rules aggrieved members can approach the organization for redress against dumping and discriminatory tariff practices of another country. It will be difficult for Pakistan to resist the pressures for expanded trade.

The following mutually reinforcing factors would help create an environment in which a momentum for peace can be generated:

(*a*) The growing global demand for nuclear disarmament and peace, which also set up the conducive conditions around the Middle East peace process;

(*b*) International trends are encouraging globalisation and liberalisation of economies. These factors, combined with the likelihood of sub-regional groupings developing under the aegis of SAARC, provide opportunities that Pakistan can only ignore at its own peril. Therefore, discouraging trade with India runs counter to Pakistan's national interest since large benefits are expected to flow from such enhanced trade.

(*c*) The new generation of Pakistanis is conscious of the debilitating impact on economic growth and the diversion of a huge amount of resources to finance the cost of defence for maintaining even the present levels of security expenditure.

(*d*) Deference to the US and other western countries whose political and economic support is important for Pakistan's development who would like Pakistan to have meaningful negotiations with India.

Role of NGOs

Non-governmental initiatives are more likely to help bring the peoples of South Asia closer to each other, thereby creating conditions for developing a better understanding of each others concerns, aspirations and expectations. It is envisaged that the non-official dialogues between concerned citizens on both sides of the border would bridge the communication gap and create public opinion for narrowing differences of opinion and presenting alternatives for resolving long-standing issues.

Meanwhile, the helpful roles played by the national Chambers of Commerce and Industry and the SAARC Chamber, and the activities of NGOs in general, have been very encouraging. The commendable role played by India-Pakistan-Peoples-Forum to bring together common citizens and its summer schools to foster and actively promote understanding between the youth in these two countries is particularly noteworthy. However, these efforts and achievements are neutralised by the extremely slow pace of co-operation in South Asia because of the structural and administrative impediments to people-to-people contact.

RECOMMENDATIONS BUILDING ON PROPOSALS EMANATING FROM SAARC

The first set of recommendations seek to build on the beginnings already made since the formation of SAARC:

- The ambit of the Visa Exemption Scheme should be expanded. Through negotiations and mutually agreed mechanisms, more categories of individuals—for example, professionals like accountants, doctors, engineers, journalists, and academics—should be covered by the scheme.
- The SAARC scheme relating to the expansion of tourism in the region should be taken up for further discussion and steps should be initiated to ensure its speedy implementation. For a start, internationally recognised travel agencies should be issued permits enabling them to organise tours across borders.
- The mobility of senior office-bearers of well established NGOs with a credible track record should be enhanced by issuing them multiple entry open visas. To enable SAARC affiliated NGOs in SAARC to expand their activities, a SAARC fund should be set up for facilitating their interaction and dialogue. To supplement

this fund additional resources could be mobilised from international donors.

- To facilitate the interaction of traders, businessmen and ordinary citizens, industrial and commercial exhibitions should be organised along the borders. The venues for such fairs (*melas*) should be carved out from the land on both sides of the border; entries to these venues should not require visas. The two governments should actively support and participate in it.
- Senior citizens (individuals above 65 years of age) of both Pakistan and India should be allowed to travel freely across the border without any visa or prior permission.[7]
- Tours of young students should be organised during school and college vacations. To institutionalise such an initiative, both Pakistan and India should invite 500 students under the age of 15 by granting them the status of state guests.
- A speedier processing of visa applications filed with the Ministry of Interior or the Home Departments of the Provincial Governments could be facilitated through a computerised:

(*a*) database of Pakistanis falling in the divided families category; and

(*b*) record of a list of undesirables whose applications could be rejected straightaway while those of others are cleared as a routine matter.

Proposals aimed at the Enhancement of Capacity of High Commissions

The second set of recommendations are aimed at improving the functioning of the High Commissions/Embassies.

- By increasing the number of visa-related staff, the pre-verification and visa processing efforts can be conducted speedily

[7] Since the two governments are not expected to accept the free movement of people in the immediate future, it is proposed that restrictions should first be relaxed for such citizens as they are less likely to be viewed as security risks. Moreover, such individuals were uprooted from their places of birth and are eager to re-visit their homes.

and more efficiently. Applicants should also be accorded a right to receive a response to their requests within a specified time.

- The discretionary quotas with the High Commissioners should be increased, and, as a first step, this quota should be doubled.[8]
- All restrictions to issue transit visas should be lifted in the event that a flight is cancelled suddenly or when a passenger is not responsible for missing a flight.

RECOMMENDATIONS TO REMOVE THE PERCEPTUAL IMPEDIMENTS

The following set of recommendations is more broad-based and focuses on ways to remove the perceptual blockages:

- Objective factors underlie the distrust that prevails. The element of hostility and rivalry is deep-rooted. Hence, Pakistan, the smaller country feels that confidence building measures can be enhanced if India, as the major player in the region, becomes more forthcoming and magnanimous. It expects India to take the initiative and make the environment more conducive to a meaningful dialogue and a more effective people-to-people contact programme. Pakistan feels that this could be achieved if three steps were taken by India.

    (*a*) Simplify the visa procedures, introduce country visas (as distinct from the current practice of city visas) and withdraw police reporting requirements for certain categories of travellers, businessmen and accredited journalists.

    (*b*) Implement the 1988 agreement covering cultural exchange by revising textbooks of history and geography so as to remove misrepresentations about Pakistan. This objective could be achieved by inviting reputed Pakistani historians to make appropriate recommendations in this regard, in consultation with their Indian counterparts.

[8] Since changing the categories of visa-seekers requires a policy change, it would be more difficult to institute; it would qualify under the third set of recommendations.

(*c*) Invite Pakistan to re-open its consulate in the Jinnah House in Mumbai.

- Non-official dialogue between the more prominent and opinion-making segments of the polities of both countries—political leaders, parliamentarians, bureaucrats, retired military personnel, journalists and other media persons, academics, students, artists, lawyers, other professionals, human rights activists, women's rights activists and businessmen—should be encouraged. This is desirable because the government to government channels of communication which are, in any case, inadequate, have not been functioning. Initiatives like these are desirable for building a wider constituency for peace. It is hoped that such a combination of individuals and institutions will be in a position to present alternatives to the supposed nationalist foreign policy agendas of their respective governments, as well as to sensitise public opinion thereby preparing the ground for more meaningful formal negotiations between the two governments. By commencing the process with more modest objectives and initiating discussions on sensitive issues (including the core security issue of Kashmir that has, historically, bedevilled relations), supplemented by decisions to open up trade between the two countries, early successes can be achieved. Expanded opportunities for trade, in particular, should facilitate the development of a strong lobby of stake-holders for peace.
- A fair amount of goodwill has developed among common citizens of both countries with the relaxation, albeit limited, of travel restrictions. This goodwill can be harnessed by those engaged in non-official dialogue for expanding the constituency for peace so that additional pressure can be brought to bear on the respective governments to improve relations. If the body of public opinion in favour of peace and friendship can be expanded, it can acquire a vigour of its own and, eventually, be in a position to assert itself as a powerful voice.
- The two sides should resume talking to each other at an official level if old animosities and perceptions of threats to security, misapprehensions, biases, and myths are to be removed. Several myths have to be challenged, like the obstacles placed in the

path of normalisation by hostile public opinion that will view any attempt at normalisation as a 'sell-out' and not countenance any 'concessions' to the other side for improving bilateral relations. Regular contacts will particularly help develop a better understanding of reciprocal concerns. In this regard, humanitarian gestures like the release of children captured from Indian boats that strayed into Pakistani waters are to be commended. To move towards peace, a slow, sustained dialogue will have to be conducted. Since there are no short cuts, hopes for a spectacular breakthrough would be unwarranted.

- To create the environment for a successful dialogue, maximum effort should be directed at ensuring that the environment in favour of normalisation of relations is not vitiated. For instance, communiques should avoid cliches like failure of talks, deadlock, etc. This might require bringing an unprejudiced mind to the talks. Such a dialogue should initially focus on matters (such as expanded trade and Siachen) on which agreement can be reached in a short timeframe. Conscious attempts by the two governments to convince their respective peoples that they have a stake in each other's independence and prosperity are not likely to meet any popular resistance, partly due to the fact that those who talk of confrontation with India have been marginalised in Pakistan. And if, as a goodwill gesture, India were to release some imprisoned Kashmiri leaders, normalisation efforts would get a new lease of life.
- There needs to be greater interaction between government and civil society in the making of national foreign policy. Civil society is putting pressure on government and is beginning to induce marginal changes in policy and policy-making processes.
- With the expansion of satellite television territorial boundaries have been crossed. Privately managed television can, therefore, be harnessed into playing a more active and constructive role in promoting efforts directed at peace.
- The apex regional organisation of business—the SAARC Chamber of Commerce and Industry—has asked governments to work towards one SAARC-Visa for visitors from outside the region. This would facilitate access to all countries by enabling businessmen and other travellers to travel across the region. The

economic benefits to flow from such measures could be quite significant.

- The present air travel schedules do not seem to promote, if they do not positively discourage, travel within the region. There is, therefore, a need to allow more air links between the countries, especially by facilitating the operations of private airlines within the region and by extending to them the same treatment given to the national airlines, to the other airlines.
- The expansion of regional transportation arrangements will help boost intra-regional trade. Mass tourism is only possible through surface travel; therefore, the railway systems and road networks of the region have to be integrated and developed, both from the point of improving mutual relationships and the standard of infrastructure. Moreover, the movement of surface transportation has to be eased by increasing the number of border-crossing points, e.g. through the opening of the Khokrapar-Munabo rail link to facilitate travellers from the Sindh province in Pakistan.
- There is also need to encourage sponsorship of sports and cultural exchanges, including the holding of art and film festivals.
- In view of their common heritage of the British parliamentary and legal systems the countries in the region could also share their experiences on matters relating to constitutional, legal and institutional reforms.

APPENDIX I

COUNTRIES IN WHICH PAKISTAN EMBASSY ENJOYS FULL VISA ISSUING POWERS

Australia	Germany	Kuwait	Singapore
Austria	Greece	Luxembourg	South Korea
Bahrain	Hong Kong	Malaysia	Spain
Belgium	Hungary	Netherlands	Sweden
Brunei	Iceland	New Zealand	Switzerland
Canada	Indonesia	Norway	Thailand
China	Iran	Oman	Turkey
Czechoslovakia	Ireland	Poland	United Arab Emirates
Denmark	Italy	Portugal	United Kingdom
Finland	Japan	Qatar	United States of America
France	Kenya	Saudi Arabia	

People-to-People Contact in South Asia: The Case of Sri Lanka

VICTOR GUNAWARDENA

INTRODUCTION

Perhaps the earliest call for regional cooperation in South Asia came from Jawaharlal Nehru, who as India's first Prime Minister convened the Asian Relations Conference in New Delhi in 1947. He sought primarily to create an Asian consciousness on which to build viable and mutually beneficial linkages. Several similar conferences followed, which like the Nehru initiative, had a wider perspective than South Asia.

Four years after the Treaty of Rome, the precursor to the European Community and the European Common Market, was signed in 1957. The Economic Commission for Asia and the Far East (ECAFE) proposed an Asian Common Market. It was initially to promote economic cooperation and then to integration. However, the concept was rejected in 1963. Nevertheless, there resulted two significant Asian structures in the mid-1970s, the Asian Clearing Union (ACU) and the Bangkok Trade Agreement, in both of which the initiative came from South Asian nations.

At the conference which Nehru convened in 1947 he proposed among other things the setting up of an Asian Institute for the study of problems common to Asian countries. Six years later the Institute of Asian Studies was founded in Hyderabad with the aim of conducting research in historical studies and cultural relations between India and other Asian countries. Since then there has emerged a regional dimension of Asian scholarship with a focus on the development of new relationships and cooperative linkages within the region, more particularly the South Asian region.

A significant structural development which gave a vital impetus to South Asian cooperation was the setting up, in 1978, of a South Asian collectivity of scholars styled the Committee on Studies for Cooperation in Development (CSCD) with its secretariat at the Marga Institute in Colombo.

Among the fourteen studies initially undertaken in its Cooperative Research Programme was the one described as 'Living standards, consumption patterns, lifestyles and cultural values in the countries of the region and their bearing on national and regional development policies and priorities (Alternatives in Development)'. From this seminal idea grew the theme of people-to-people contact.

A further fillip to the work of the South Asian scholars engaged in research on regional cooperation came from the meeting in Colombo, in April 1981, of the Foreign Secretaries of the seven South Asian countries. It created a political framework for non-political cooperation on subjects that were then non-controversial among the respective governments. Sri Lanka's Foreign Minister, A.C.S. Hameed, in his address to the meeting stressed the need for 'a sustained programme of public information through which knowledge of each other can be shared at all levels'. Thus the political will for regional cooperation was acknowledged as an imperative, for which public information and people-to-people contact are indispensable.

Additionally, during the first phase of the CSCD programme (1978-84) priority was accorded to trade expansion and the external relations within the region primarily as a means of accelerating internal socio-economic changes and achieving development objectives as determined by the respective countries.

BANGALORE SUMMIT DIMENSIONS OF PEOPLE-TO-PEOPLE CONTACT

In the Bangalore Summit of the Heads of State of the South Asian Association for Regional Cooperation (SAARC) held in November

1986, special emphasis was given to promoting people-to-people contact in the region by adapting the following five initiatives:

I. SAARC Audio-Visual Exchange (SAVE) Programme

This was already in existence and in adapting it to establish people-to-people contact, the Summit believed it could be an effective medium for promoting South Asian consciousness among the people of the region through regular TV and radio programmes and quiz programmes.

In November 1993, a succinct criticism of the SAVE programme was made at a conference of regional scholars and policy practitioners held in Kathmandu.

The particular criticism of SAVE reads:

> The frequency of SAVE programmes should be increased from once a month to once a fortnight. Such programmes should be broadcast and telecast on fixed days of the month and at prime time. The content of the programmes needs to be enhanced and enriched by focusing also on socially sensitive issues such as poverty, environment, children, women and youth. The programme could profit from highlighting success stories in combating problems common to the region. The SAVE technical committee could be assisted in its work by media professionals including freelance producers, besides other relevant personnel.

SAVE has had little impact on Sri Lankan audiences and is hardly talked about or awaited by viewers.

On the other hand, the Young Asia television programmes screened every evening in the region establish contact among a younger generat-ion of South Asians far more effectively than SAVE's fortnightly programme. The themes and issues depicted combine information with entertainment and make contact with people both realistically and imaginatively in dealing with live social and cultural issues.

II. SAARC Documentation Centre (SDC)

Although the Centre was established to provide ready access to reliable and up-to-date information on technical and scientific and development matters, scholars in the region lament that the accumulated data are not easily available in the national SAARC documentation systems (SDS).

For instance, the reports and other documents of the Integrated Programme of Action (IPA) are not available at the Sri Lanka SAARC documentation centre; nor are they available for reference by scholars and media personnel.

Consequently, little is known within Member States about the IPA, which is central to the SAARC process on the eleven agreed areas of cooperation. To that extent contact among people in the region who are especially interested in the various processes of development, particularly in science and technology, is restricted.

III. SAARC Scheme for Promotion of Organised Tourism

The scheme was introduced with the overall objective of promoting people-to-people contact in the region and specifically to facilitate development of intra-regional tourism. The scheme was to provide inter alia for concessional air fare to tourists travelling under the scheme. However, there was no reference to the scheme in the Dhaka Declaration (April 1993) nor in the Delhi Declaration (May 1995).

The Male Declaration (May 1997) also makes no reference to the scheme but carries two paragraphs on tourism and makes the point that organised tourism in the region 'has not yet achieved its full potential', and recommends that 'appropriate measures to promote tourism be given priority'. The Summit was convinced that 'greater cooperation in this area would contribute to the enhancement of people-to-people contact within the region as well as to the economic development of Member States'.

A positive development at the Male Summit was the decision that the respective civil aviation authorities 'should meet in the very near future with a view to establishing direct air services between SAARC capitals which would promote people-to-people contact and encourage tourism'.

At present the absence of such direct air services—between

Kathmandu and Islamabad, Colombo and Kathmandu, and between Dhaka and Islamabad, and Colombo and Dhaka—obliges the traveller to go via a third country, often breaking journey and experiencing the hassle of border formalities including transit visas, customs declarations, and inspection of baggage.

A significant omission in the scheme for promoting intra-regional travel is the absence of separate immigration counters for SAARC country passport-holders. Although SAARC has been in operation for over a decade, citizens of the Association's Member States do not have a common identity which would entitle them to special treatment at airports and other points of transborder entry and exit. Invariably, they are required to join queues for foreigners at the airports of the countries they visit in the region. The hassle and delays they experience are by no means conducive to promoting people-to-people contact and tend to spoil their first impressions of the host country.

A human factor that has been overlooked in efforts to promote people-to-people contact through travel within the region is the absence of concern for the convenience of applicants seeking a visa to travel to another country in the region. This is most evident outside the offices of the Indian and Pakistan High Commissions in Colombo. Would-be-travellers to either country are obliged to stand in queues outside the respective offices, often exposed to the elements, and await their turn for their visa applications to be processed. Respect for human dignity requires that proper shelter and a waiting hall be provided for applicants while they wait for the transaction of business.

It must, however, be noted that prominent businessmen, government officials and private sector personnel seeking to obtain visas from either High Commission do not have to go through the ordeal of standing in a queue outside the office. They visit the office by appointment and meet the visa officer direct but for the 'ordinary traveller' the ordeal of queues and delays seems inevitable.

It is this absence of a human face in the Member States' official procedures and attitudes that compounds the compounds the constraints that the would-be 'ordinary traveller' to a country in the region has to put up with. People-to-people contact in the South Asian context is thereby vitiated at the very outset of a proposed journey to a neighbouring country.

IV. SAARC Chairs, Fellowships and Scholarships Scheme (*SCFSS*)

The SCFSS scheme aims at promoting increased cross-fertilisation of ideas through greater interaction among students, scholars and academics in SAARC. The scheme has been functioning since 1994 under the purview of the Technical Committee on Education and Culture.

The SAARC Chairs, Fellowships and Scholarships Scheme received some publicity in Sri Lanka when Professor Shelton Kodikara, a reputed political scientist from Sri Lanka, was appointed to the first SAARC Chair of Political Science at Jawaharlal Nehru University in New Delhi. But with his demise in 1995 little is known here about the scheme.

The Male Summit was of the view that the scheme 'should be increasingly used to facilitate greater interaction among students, scholars and academics in the region'. However, information is not easily available on whether this is being done.

V. SAARC Youth Volunteers Programme (SYVOP)

SYVOP was brought under the purview of the Technical Committee on Rural Development. It seeks 'to harness the idealism of youth for regional cooperation programmes by enabling them to work in other countries in the field of agriculture and forestry extension work'.

Nevertheless, there was no reference at all to SYVOP in the Declarations of the past three Summits since—Dhaka, Delhi and Male. However, two significant events occurred in 1994. One was that 1994 was designated as the SAARC Year of the Youth. The other was the adoption of a Resolution on youth by the Ministerial Conference on Youth in South Asia held in Male in May 1994. One of the results was the establishment of the SAARC Youth Awards

Scheme, which, according to the Male Declaration, has been operationalised. There is also an initiative to organise youth camps in the region on various themes.

REVIEW OF THE FIVE INITIATIVES

The foregoing comments on the five initiatives or mechanisms which the Bangalore Summit of 1986 approved as a means of promoting people-to-people contact in the region would indicate that the SAARC perception of each as part of a strategy to achieve a declared objective has changed over the years.

Firstly, there has been inadequate publicity in Sri Lanka about the five initiatives as part of a strategy to promote people-to-people contact. It would appear that information about the five schemes has been confined within the Foreign Ministry and that very little planned promotional work has been done towards achieving the specific objectives.

Of the five schemes, SAVE gained some visibility in Sri Lanka because it was screened during a period of prime viewing. The criticisms of SAVE that were brought to the notice of the SAARC Secretariat appear to have gone unheeded.

The promotion of people-to-people contact requires a sustained programme of public information about each of the mechanisms which comprise the strategy. Further, each scheme needs to be monitored in each country and in the region by the SAARC Secretariat or by a particular Technical Committee.

A careful reading of the respective Summit Declarations on people-to-people contact reveals the recurrence of vague rhetoric seeking to express satisfaction with what SAARC put in place. However, it is significant to note that three Summit Declarations mention the role of the SAARC Chamber of Commerce and Industry and SAARC LAW as having positively contributed to strengthening mutual understanding and goodwill among people in the region.

Both organisations are non-governmental āpex professional bodies in the region. Similarly, other apex bodies of accountants, architects and university women have applied for official SAARC recognition of their *de facto apex* status, which is conducive to promoting people-to-people contact besides furthering their particular interests in the countries of the region.

It would thus appear that such non-governmental professional bodies have done much more towards achieving the objectives of people-to-people contact than the official mechanisms of SAARC. Therefore, expression of satisfaction with the people-to-people contact scheme as recorded in the respective Summit Declarations must be interpreted as reflecting the work of the non-governmental apex professional bodies referred to earlier.

SRI LANKA'S DIPLOMATIC RELATIONS IN SOUTH ASIA

Sri Lanka has diplomatic relations with its other SAARC member states, but it has no resident mission in Bhutan nor has that country a resident mission in Colombo. Bhutan's Ambassador to New Delhi (resident there) is also accredited to Colombo. Likewise, Sri Lanka's High Commissioner to New Delhi is also accredited to Thimpu. All other SAARC member states have resident missions in Colombo and Sri Lanka has reciprocal diplomatic relations. However, Nepal had only a Consul-General till 1995, when that country appointed a resident Ambasador in Colombo, reciprocating Sri Lanka's gesture. Earlier, Sri Lanka's High Commissioner to Dhaka was also accredited to Kathmandu. At present, there is a full-fledged Sri Lankan mission in Kathmandu.

For historical and trade reasons Sri Lanka has, besides its High Commissioner in New Delhi, a Deputy High Commissioner in Madras and a Trade Consulate in Mumbai (Bombay). India has its High Commissioner and Deputy in Colombo as well as an Assistant High Commissioner stationed in Kandy. The latter posting goes back to the early 1830s with the introduction of Indian immigrant labour to the plantations.

Sri Lanka has its High Commissioner in Islamabad and a Trade Commissioner in Karachi. Thus, India and Pakistan have a wider interest in their diplomatic relations with Sri Lanka, which are reciprocated. Bangladesh and the Maldives maintain the normal diplomatic relations. Nepal holds a special interest for Sri Lankan travellers of whom 90 per cent are pilgrims to Buddhist places of interest, in particular Lumbini.

SOME LEGAL AND ADMINISTRATIVE IMPEDIMENTS TO TRAVEL BETWEEN SRI LANKA AND COUNTRIES IN THE REGION

Sri Lankan travel documents, such as passport and emergency certificates, are issued to Sri Lankan nationals under the provisions of the Immigrants and Emigrants Act. No. 20 of 1948 and as subsequently amended. The Act came into operation on 1 November 1948 and is referred to as Chapter 351 in the Legislative Enactments of Ceylon (Sri Lanka since 1972), Revised Edition, 1956.

The Act provides for controlling entry into the Island of persons other than its own citizens, for regulating the departure from the Island of its citizens and persons other than citizens, for removing from the Island undesirable persons who are not citizens of Sri Lanka, and for other matters incidental to or connected therewith.

Passports are issued to Sri Lankan citizens and are valid for a period of five years, renewable for a further period of five years.

Entry to Sri Lanka is permitted to Sri Lankan citizens who are in possession of valid travel documents. Non-citizens are permitted entry only if they are in possession of valid passports and visas or valid Residence Visas or are granted endorsements at the port of entry as bona fide tourists.

Residence Visas are issued by the Controller of Immigration and Emigration at his discretion, for purposes of employment, study, holiday, etc., provided the entry to and stay in the Island of such persons is not prejudicial to the interests of the permanent inhabitants of the Island.

Visit Visas, permitting stay in the Island up to a maximum period of six months, are issued by the Controller of Immigration and Emigration and Sri Lanka's accredited representatives overseas. Extensions of visas are granted by the Controller.

Endorsements permitting entry to and stay in the Island for a period not exceeding one month are granted by authorised officers at ports of entry to citizens of certain specified countries provided their stay in the Island does not exceed one month. Such persons must have with them sufficient foreign exchange for their maintenance during their stay and also possess a ticket for their outward journey or sufficient foreign exchange for the purchase of such a ticket. Certain categories of persons are exempted from the requirements of being in possession of visas.

Visas are not required by Sri Lankan citizens travelling to the Maldives for a purpose other than employment. This measure is reciprocal for Maldivian citizens visiting Sri Lanka. However, in either case the duration of stay is limited.

In addition to the foregoing provisions all persons disembarking at a port of entry to Sri Lanka must hand in Disembarkation Card giving particulars inter alia about that person's nationality, occupation and purpose of visit.

There are seven categories of purpose: (i) Transit; (ii) Holiday; (iii) Business; (iv) Employment; (v) Conference; (vi) Visiting Friends/ Relations; and (vii) Others.

Likewise, all passengers embarking on their journey out of the Island must fill an Embarkation Card giving particulars about themselves and the purpose of travel abroad.

Purpose is categorised as follows: (i) Vacation, (ii) Business, (iii) Studies (iv) Employmen, and (v) Others.

Applicants for visas to travel to Sri Lanka for a purpose such as business, studies or employment may be required to provide documentary evidence to support the stated purpose of the proposed visit. If the officer authorised to issue the visa is not satisfied that the applicant has a bona fide purpose he may exercise his discretion to refuse to issue a visa.

Such a procedure is reciprocal in respect of Sri Lankan visa applicants wishing to travel to other countries. In the South Asian region there are procedural constraints to the issue of visas for reasons of national security and to counter terrorist activities, drug offences and smuggling. There is evidence of couriers travelling between some countries in the region purportedly for a bona fide purpose, but in fact to further an illegal activity. Besides the smuggling of narcotics there is also evidence of gold and currency smuggling by ostensibly bona fide travellers. Further, there, is evidence in Sri Lanka of persons travelling to and from certain countries in the region on forged travel documents.

With the liberalisation of the economy in each of the South Asian countries there has been a rapid expansion of the private sector and many small business establishments and commission agents have mushroomed in Sri Lanka in addition to the expansion of business of the established commercial and trading houses.

INFORMATION FROM FEDERATION OF CHAMBERS OF COMMERCE AND INDUSTRY OF SRI LANKA (FCCISL)

Owing to the high visibility of the latter group by reason of their standing in the business community their members reportedly do not encounter much difficulty in obtaining visas for business travel within the region. Information gathered from the office of the Federation of Chambers of Commerce and Industry of Sri Lanka (FCCISL) in respect of the business-related travel of its members within the region confirms that:

(*a*) Members of the Executive Committee of the SAARC Chambers of Commerce and Industry (SCCI) are issued with a multiple entry visa valid for one year from the date of issue by the country in the region which they intend to visit.

(*b*) Members of the FCCISL who wish to travel to India are issued with a single entry visa valid for a limited period depending on the purpose of the visit. Generally the period of validity is six months.

(*c*) There is a similar provision in respect of travel to Pakistan.

(*d*) Bangladesh issues a multiple entry visa valid for one year for business travel.

(*e*) Nepal issues a multiple entry visa valid for 60 days for all purposes. However, Nepalis wishing to travel to Sri Lanka on business are issued with a single entry visa valid for only 30 days.

The Nepal Mission in Colombo was opened only in May 1995. Its fiscal year is from July to June. Its issue of visas began in July 1995 and in the first year of the Mission's functioning 10,604 visas were issued, 90 per cent of them for the purpose of pilgrimage.

The mission has no separate data on visas for business travel. The visa application categories are:

i. Official, i.e. sponsored by both governments,
ii. Tourist,
iii. Pilgrimage, and
iv. Others

(*f*) Travel to the Maldives. No visas are ordinarily required.
(*g*) Bhutan—issue of visas for business travel does not arise.

Additionally, information was also available on the facilitating role played by the FCCISL in promoting SAARC Chamber (SCCI) activities during the year 1996.

The FCCISL organised a delegation of 30 private sector businessmen including members of three Sri Lankan Chambers who participated in the first SAARC Trade Fair held in New Delhi from 9 to 14 January 1996.

Also in January, FCCISL members of the SCCI Executive Committee attended a meeting in New Delhi. Between March and July 1996 FCCISL members actively participated in the second round of Trade Negotiations under SAPTA and submitted proposals to be taken up at the Inter-Governmental group meeting at Lahore.

In August and October 1995 FCCISL members participated in the first SCCI tourism council seminar in Lahore and the third such seminar in New Delhi.

The second SCCI seminar in the series was held in Colombo in September 1995.

The FCCISL also participated in the SAARC Economic Cooperation Conference organised by the SCCI and FICCI and held in New Delhi in November 1996.

The foregoing information suggests that organised business travel in the region under the auspices of representative bodies in the trade and commerce sectors does not experience the hassle and restrictions complained of by individual businessmen who seek to travel to one or other country in the region.

VIEW OF THE INDIAN HIGH COMMISSION

Information gathered from the Indian High Commission suggests that bona fide Sri Lankan businessmen whose credentials have been established and who seek to travel to India on business have little difficulty in obtaining visas, generally valid for a period of six months.

However, the High Commission's difficulties arise mainly in dealing with Sri Lankan nationals claiming to be businessmen who wish to travel often to India within a year. Officials are wary about various ruses that some such applicants resort to, giving rise to suspicion that the declared purpose of travel to India may not genuinely be business. The suspicion grows that some such persons may be illicit couriers or smugglers acting on behalf of persons who fund their travel. Suspicion is reinforced when some such applicants for visas report loss of their earlier travel documents which would contain evidence of their previous travel to India, and make their fresh applications for visas on new passports.

A peculiarity of the Indian visa application form is that the category 'business' is inclusive of such activities as conferences and seminars which are not necessarily business-oriented. As a result it is difficult to collect statistics on actual business travel as distinct from travel on other work, whether official or non-official.

The volume and frequency of travel by Sri Lankans to India for the stated purpose of travel exceed by far travel to any other country in the region. Actual figures, however, are not easily obtainable but the conclusion is verifiable from the Sri Lankan Immigration and Emigration Department's data.

Overall, the foregoing indicates the absence of the principle of reciprocity relating to the issue of visas by the respective countries. Sri Lanka, however, does not have the kind of problem vis-à-vis any particular country that India and Pakistan have towards each other.

President, National Chamber of Commerce, Sri Lanka Armyne Wirasinha opined that over the past decade, whilst some effort was made to improve economic and trading ties within the region, the results have not been too encouraging. He feels, on the other hand, had there been expansion of trade, joint ventures, etc., intra-country business travel would have been greater.

According to Mr Wirasinha, foundations for the development of business travel within the South Asia Region will quite obviously depend on the expansion of business and inter-country trading and investment as well as collaboration. This is an essential pre-requisite.

Whilst initiatives have been made for the strengthening of economic ties, in reality these attempts are only recent. Many countries within this region had earlier thought in terms of regional cooperation from an Asian perspective and not from the point of view of the sub-region. Thus SAARC is a belated development in sub-regional cooperation.

Intra-trade between the SAARC nations is approximately 3 to 4 % of their total world trade. Trade within the region is also not expanding. A similar sub-regional effort, the Bangkok Agreement formed in 1978 for the purpose of Asian Trade Cooperation has not unfortunately had the desired impact.

To intensify trade cooperation would imply the granting of tariff concessions for products on a multilateral basis. Though several meetings have been held recently with regard to both bi-lateral and multilateral tariff concessions, there does not seem to be much improvement in the overall trading position within the region.

The ultimate objective of regional cooperation for the development of business travel should examine the possibility of a free trade area. Indeed this has already been discussed and initiated but the preferential arrangements for tariff concessions seem to be in a state of flux and as a consequence a Free Trade Area looks only a remote possibility.

The expansion of trade and investment plus joint ventures are definite measures of increasing business travel. But quite apart from India and Pakistan, the new initiatives through SAARC have not opened up fresh avenues of trade within the member nations. For example a SAARC

Chamber of Commerce and Industry has been established and Sri Lanka has two member institutions within this Chamber. They are also represented on the Council, which is the governing body of the SAARC Chamber of Commerce. It should be a primary task of this Institution to create a trade consciousness among member nations, promote opportunities for greater intra-country trade amongst the business community, conduct regional and market studies and also encourage individual tie-ups between the businesses of the respective countries. Such developments would indeed pave the way for greater travel between representatives of business houses.

The SAARC Chambers have various ad hoc committees that examine sectoral developments within the region. A particular area of attention should be the establishment of a relatively easy travel regime that includes concessionary hotel rates, as well as preferential air fares and frequent flights for business travel. Such concessions should also apply to members of Chambers of Commerce within the community of SAARC. It is also suggested that the airlines of SAARC countries and the travel agents/tour operators in the respective countries form themselves into an association essentially to structure and implement a suitable and effective programme that would facilitate and generate interest in travel within the SAARC region. Such an association could thus meaningfully address the several issues involved in developing and promoting inter-country travel within the seven nations of SAARC.

It is important to appoint country representatives in each of the seven SAARC nations who would examine all aspects of trade, their constraints and investments as well as business travel for the consideration of the Council of SAARC. A joint quarterly publication should be issued containing precise reports from each country giving travel prospects and other similar information.

In the wider interest of the SAARC nations, each state or region should have a Honorary Consular Officer or a Consul General who could play a useful role in promoting business-related travel.

There is evidently a much-felt need for more bi-lateral trade associations to be formed. At present the Sri Lankan business community have only about three such tie-ups with India and Pakistan.

A Sri Lanka-Nepal Business Cooperation Council is in the process of being established. Since trade between these two countries has increased substantially in the last few years this council should indeed help promote the development of trade and consequently business travel. Nepal is an attractive destination for tourists from the region and combined pleasure/ business visits are likely to follow if an institution is able to guide and support trade.

Similar institutional arrangements with other countries of our region with whom we have very little arrangements of this nature should encourage business travel.

Visa exemption schemes within the region are a key factor but establishment of a scheme of this nature has of necessity to examine carefully the credentials of each business visitor. Our region is prominent for illegal activities like drug trafficking and terrorism. A visa exemption scheme has obviously to take into consideration advice and support of various Chambers of Commerce of the region, especially for ensuring the bona fides of prospective business travellers.

Regional bodies like SAARC need leadership. The success achieved by ASEAN is as a consequence of the Japanese leadership and interest in investments, trade, and most trade complementaries afforded on mutually acceptable concessions. Japan also led the way in creating sub-regional schemes of technical assistance and research within the five-nation ASEAN. The resultant economic developments in the past ten years were rapid and business travel within the region expanded equally rapidly. SAARC should follow suit and have one of its bigger partners to take the lead in generating an environment of business and travel growth.

Quite apart from existing travel barriers like visa difficulties, enhancement of air capacity, it is primarily sub-regional business cooperation and its practical developments that will help travel promotion amongst the business community.'

SAARC VISA EXEMPTION SCHEME

The Visa Exemption Scheme among SARC countires was initiated in 1988 in order to promote closer and more frequent contacts among the peoples of the region. The scheme became operational from 1 March 1992. Up to two years later 773 persons had availed themselves of the scheme and five years after its operation a total of 1,600 persons had been issued visas under it.

Initially, those entitled to the facility were judges of the Supreme Court, members of national Parliaments, heads of national academic institutions and their accompanying spouses and dependent children.

The scheme was later extended to include Foreign/Permanent Secretaries dealing with foreign affairs, the SAARC Secretary-General and Directors of the SAARC Secretariat, Presidents of national Chambers of Commerce and Industry. The scheme covers also the accompanying spouses and dependent children under 18 years of age.

Extension of the Scheme had been recommended to successive Summits by the Standing Committee and the Council of Ministers. In particular, it was urged that officials in the governmental sector and office-bearers in the non-governmental sector dealing with trade and economic cooperation be also included in the Scheme.

The Male Summit in May 1997 accepted the recommendations and increased the number of categories that are entitled to the facility to 21. Originally the entitlement was limited to the first three categories in the list appearing below.

The following is the consolidated list of categories of entitled persons under the SAARC Visa Exemption Scheme:

(*a*) Supreme Court Judges.
(*b*) Members of National Parliaments.
(*c*) Heads of National Academic Institutions.
(*d*) Foreign/Permanent Secretaries dealing with Foreign Affairs.
(*e*) SAARC Secretary-General.
(*f*) Directors of the SAARC Secretariat.
(*g*) Presidents of National Chambers of Commerce and Industry.
(*h*) Permanent Secretaries in Trade Ministries and up to three othe officials concerned with promotion of intra-SAARC trade and economic cooperation from each Member State as nominated by them.
(*i*) Vice Presidents and Members of the Executive Committee of the SAARC Chamber of Commerce and Industry.
(j) Members of the Executive Committee of the National Federations of Chambers of Commerce and Industry.
(*k*) Members of SAPTA Committee of Participants.
(*l*) All Central Government Ministers/Ministers of State/Deputy Ministers/Assistant Ministers in Member States.

(*m*) Secretaries/Administrative Heads of Ministries of equiva lent rank dealing with the subjects handled by eleven SAARC Technical Committees.

(*n*) Secretaries involved in the SAARC three-tier poverty alleviation mechanism—Finance, Planning, Rural Development, Urban Development.

(*o*) Heads of National Radio and TV Organisations.

(*p*) Heads of National Sports Authorities and Federations.

(*q*) Chairmen of National and International Airlines.

(*r*) Heads of National Academies and Institutions in the field of Art and Culture, and of National Museums.

(*s*) Heads of Boards of Customs and Revenue.

(*t*) SAARC National Focal Points (Heads of SAARC Divisions of Ministries of Foreign/External Affairs).

(*u*) President and Vice-Presidents of SAARC LAW.

The spouses and dependent children below 18 years of age accompanying the above categories of persons will also be entitled to the SAARC Visa Exemption Scheme.

Note: Categories of persons in this list were included in a chronological order in which they were approved for inclusion in the list.

All such eligible persons are entitled to have the special visa exemption stickers available with the respective Foreign Offices or the SAARC Secretariat pasted on their passports.

Nevertheless, criticism of the operation of the Scheme is mainly that its particulars have not been published in the Member States. Consequently, not enough relevant information appears to be available among the consular sections of the missions in the region as well as immigration officials handling transborder visa applications.

In the confusion about the scope of eligibility under the scheme even persons entitled to exemption under the initial category are themselves unaware of the fact and apply for travel visas following the normal procedure.

It is unfortunate that such persons are put to inconvenience and delays despite their proclaimed and eligibility for visa exemption.

According to some foreign mission consular officers this happens because the respective Foreign Offices have not given adequate publicity to this Scheme.

For instance, the 1997 Male Summit Declaration contained the bald declaration that:

> The Heads of States or Government noted with satisfaction the inclusion of new categories of persons from different walks of life in the SAARC Visa Exemption Scheme and believed that this would further promote people-to-people contact.

The Statement contains no indication that the new consolidated list contains 21 categories, a major extension from the original three.

In Sri Lanka the Foreign Office apparently did not consider it important enough to publicise the fact and detail the new categories. It would appear that the information has been withheld from the media too. The media in our respective countries do not ordinarily have access to reports of the Standing Committee and cannot therefore be expected to publicise information in the possession of the Foreign Office.

The fact draws attention to the absence of a relevant and sustained information policy aimed specifically at promoting people-to-people contact. As a consequence of such a lacuna, and due to ignorance on the part of the relevant officials, persons who are eligible to visa exemption may be deprived of that facility. This could have vexatious repercussions which would vitiate the scheme, intended to promote people-to-people contact and closer cooperation in achieving the objectives of SAARC.

It is significant that the Visa Exemption Scheme, even in its expanded form has a bias towards the governmental sector. Civil society is inadequately provided for except for the inclusion of office-bearers of representative organisations of commerce and industry. Of the other apex organisations, only SAARC LAW has provision for its President and Vice-President. In the sphere of media only heads of national radio and TV organisations are eligible. Despite the posturing towards civil society and non-governmental organisations there appears to be reluctance to extend to them the facility of visa exemption travel.

POLICY OPTIONS FOR FACILITATING BUSINESS-RELATED TRAVEL

1. The classification 'business' in visa application forms must be a distinct category and not be included in other categories such as conferences. Such a distinct category could facilitate official promotion of business-related travel supported by relevant documents.
2. The absence of reciprocity among Member States in the policy relating to the issue of visas is a major constraint in promoting travel within the region, especially when the purpose of travel is to further economic cooperation. Differential policies could lead to misunderstanding arising from ad hoc decisions that may seem arbitrary. A policy of reciprocity is essential for good relations among member states and for the success of efforts at people-to-people contact. In particular, business-related travel could be promoted if a uniform, reciprocal policy which provides for a multiple entry visa valid for one year is adopted.
3. Procedural and administrative delays in granting visas need to be eliminated. So also the inconvenience caused to applicants by long waits in queues outside consular offices exposed to the elements.
4. The Male Summit decision to explore the establishment of direct air services between SAARC capitals is a positive policy development which would go a long way to reduce the irksome and dilatory character of cross-border travel in the region.
5. The recognition of a SAARC identity for passport-holders of Member States and the provision of separate immigration counters for such SAARC citizens would considerably ease delays now experienced at ports of entry and exit in the countries of the region.
6. The absence of a clearly articulated and sustained policy of information and a strategy of implementation of the five initiatives that were approved at the Bangalore Summit of 1986 as means of promoting people-to-people contact are perceived as serious constraints.

7. An attitudinal change is also called for on the part of the respective Foreign Offices to recognise the positive and complementary role that civil society and the media could play in promoting people-to-people contact in the South Asian region.

Index